Karen Kay Buckley

# Earthly Delights
## The Perfect Finish

by Karen Kay Buckley

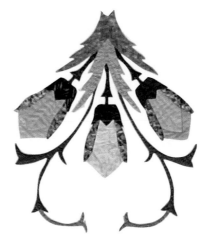

**Editors**
One of my favorite quotes is from Epictetu. "The key is to keep company only with people who uplift you, whose presence calls forth your best." All of the editors listed below do that for me.

Barbara Schenck
Lytle Markham
Joseph Buckley
Margaret Senft
Kim Thomas
Cheryl Bennecoff

**Photography**

Dan Shay - Karen Kay Buckley

**Book Design**

 Meg Ream Design, Inc.
5000 Ritter Road, Suite 202
Mechanicsburg, PA 17055

Copyright © 2006 Karen Kay Buckley, Carlisle, PA
ISBN 1-4243-0593-4

Printed in the USA through Fry Communications.

**Acknowledgements**
Thanks to all of my friends and students who encourage me to do more and better. Thank you to Joe, Kim and Lytle for your help with the photography. I could never have done it without you. You are the best.

## Dedication

For Joe
Thanks for your love and support.

# Contents

# Introduction

I have been quilting for over 20 years. I love what I do. I consider myself very lucky in that my quilts have received recognition and graced the covers of many magazines. I read a wonderful quote from Oprah, "Luck is preparation meeting opportunity. If you hadn't been prepared when the opportunity came along, you wouldn't have been lucky." Even though I have been very lucky along my journey, it is because I have worked very hard to improve with each and every quilt I make.

After presenting a lecture on quilting and showing several of my quilts to a group in New York, I asked if there were any questions. A lady in the audience said, "I don't have a question, but I do have a comment." I must admit I was a little worried what she was going to say. She said, "The borders on your quilts are amazing. You really should consider doing a lecture on how you decide on a border and how you design your borders." On the drive home from New York, I could not get this out of my mind. I kept

thinking...what an excellent idea!  Then, I started thinking of all the quilts I had made and how unique the borders were on each quilt.  I have been challenging myself for many years to do something different on each and every border but still have it complement the center design.  I gathered several of my quilts and started to present a lecture on the subject of borders.  After my lecture I am often asked if I have a book which includes all of the quilts that I had shown.  Well, that got me thinking....  This book is a compilation of the quilts I have made and the lessons I have learned.

My hope is that this book will give you some ideas.  It is not possible to offer every solution on how to finish the edge of your quilt.  But these pages will offer you lots and lots of ideas and give you the courage to design your own border which will complement your quilt to give you the perfect finish.

*Karen*

# Border Design

Before starting to sew any part of a quilt, you can decide to border or not to border. However, I like to wait until the center portion is finished. It allows the quilt to speak to me, and gives me time to contemplate what I want to do to enhance the center.

If you decide to add a border it should complement but not overwhelm, overpower or compete with the center portion of the quilt. The key to a good border is continuity of color and design from the center portion of the quilt.

Your border/borders can make or break your project. Your borders should not be an afterthought. Borders are a design element and require a lot of thought.

# Choices

1. Do you need a border? Not all quilts need a border. Some quilts look wonderful just the way they are. Sometimes simplicity is better. The first several quilts that you see in the gallery do not have borders, nor do I feel they need a border. Finishing the quilt without a border was the perfect solution.

2. Reasons to add a border:
   a. to complement the center by color and design
   b. to frame the edge
   c. to enclose the center design
   d. to balance the center
   e. to increase the size to fit the bed/wall

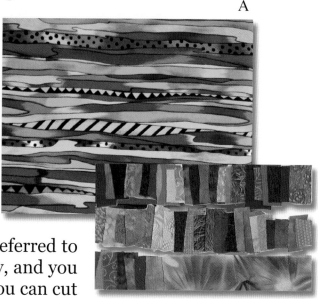

A

B

3. Should you sew first or sketch first? Neither is a bad choice, but in most cases I prefer to sketch. I like to know what is going to happen and how I can make things fit. I prefer to sketch on table paper. Table paper is not expensive. It is the type of paper you sit on in the doctor's office. It is sometimes referred to as exam paper. It is thin so it folds accurately, and you can see through it. Since it comes on a roll, you can cut the paper as one piece and do not have to tape several pieces together to get the length you need.

4. Selecting fabric for the <u>entire quilt</u>. I often work with a multi-colored print fabric that contains colors I like. If you like the colors combined in the fabric, you will love those colors combined in a quilt. The pictures above show the multi-colored theme fabric (A) and swatches of all the fabrics (B) that were used in the making of Sunny Side Up which appears on page 130.

A  B

These are the swatches (B) and the multi-colored theme fabric (A) used in Midnight Floral Fantasy which appears on page 126.

Your borders will benefit by repeating the colors used in the center of the quilt. This will give the quilt balance and continuity. You could use lighter or darker values or possibly muted or brighter shades. Introducing colors that were not used in the center may add confusion. Using a fabric that is not in the middle part of the quilt but has the same colors could work well. Generally darker colors used on the border will contain the center part of the quilt. The focus will be inside the borders.

One time I selected the colors for a quilt based on the colors in my multi-colored print fabric. I fell in love with this piece of fabric and thought it would make a great border. But when I cut a strip and placed it along the edge of the quilt center, it was too busy and detracted from the center. I pulled that fabric from the design board and made another selection. Don't be afraid to change your mind.

# Types of Borders

1. Single band of fabric
   - Plain borders are a great frame for a busy or intricate center design.
     It gives the eye a place to rest and can be a great space for some beautiful quilting.
2. Multiple bands
   - If doing more than one band/strip and you are planning to miter the corners, it is a good idea to sew all the strips together and then miter the corners. Do not miter them individually.
   - If doing more than one border strip, it is appealing to make them different widths. Don't make them all the same size.
3. Pieced
4. Appliquéd
5. Combination of pieced and appliquéd

# Miters or Straight Seams in the Borders

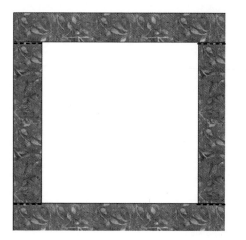

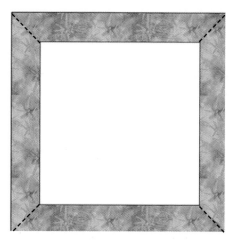

a. Straight seams, single band

b. Straight seams, corner blocks

c. Mitered corners

# Measuring to Determine the Length of Your Borders

For a square quilt follow these steps:

1. Using a 120" tape measure, measure all four edges of the quilt.
2. Write these four measurements on a piece of paper.
3. Add these four and divide by four.  The number you get will be the length of your border.  It may mean easing some fabric on some sides.  Ideally, all four sides should measure the same, but that has never happened to me.  Fabric has give.
   a. Straight seams: cut two of your strips the average length and two the average length plus two times the width.
   b. Corner blocks: cut all four borders the average length.
   c. Mitered: cut your strips the average length plus two times the width for all four strips.

**Note:** To all of these strips, no matter which border style you select, I recommend adding 3 to 4 extra inches to your average.  I would rather have a little extra at the end of the strip and have to trim it than to come up short.

4. Assume your average for a square quilt is 50".  Fold your border strip in half to find the center.  Place the 120" tape measure with the 25" line on this center crease.  Mark the back of the border strip at 0" and 50".
5. Pin the border to the quilt top matching the center 25" mark on the border with the center of the quilt top.  Place a pin at the 0" mark on one corner and the 50" mark on the other corner.  Load the edge with pins, and take it to the sewing machine.  If you are planning to do mitered borders, you must stop and start ¼" from the edges of your quilt top.  (More on this later.)
6. It is easier to sew with the fuller side against the feed dogs, letting the sewing machine ease the fit.

For a rectangular quilt, take the average of the 2 short sides and then the average of the two long sides.

# Rules or No Rules

There are no rules for how wide your borders should be, and I don't think you want them. You are better without a rule. Go with what feels right. Trust your instincts. I often fold some fabric and place it up on the design board along the center part of the quilt. By folding it in different widths I can get a good read on whether or not it is working. After putting the fabric along the edge of the quilt center, stand back. You need to back away from the project to really see the whole picture. Look through a reducing glass, camera, opposite side of a pair of binoculars, etc. This will give you a good read on what is happening. There is no reason to cut the fabric until you make the decision.

# Mitering the Borders

1/4" Mark

If you have more than one border, sew the strips together first. Then miter all the strips at one time. (I tried it the other way one time. Not a good idea!)

1. You must stop and start your sewing exactly 1/4" from the edge of the quilt top. To be sure you are exactly at the 1/4" you can draw a line 1/4" from each side corner.

2. Many of the new 1/4" patchwork feet designed for sewing machines have notches or marks along the edge to eliminate drawing on the fabric. If you place the back notch along the raw edge and the side of the foot along the other raw edge, the needle will go into the fabric exactly 1/4" from both sides. When the front notch meets the raw edge stop sewing and you will be exactly 1/4" from the corner.

3. At both the point where you start and where you finish sewing, take 3 to 4 backstitches to secure the seam.

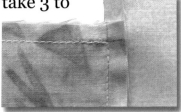

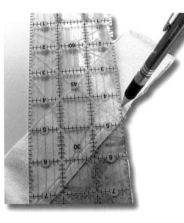

4. Fold the quilt diagonally so the right sides of the border strips are together and aligned. Place a long ruler along the fold with the 45-degree angle of the ruler along the outer raw edge and the long side of the ruler intersecting with the seam where you stopped sewing. Draw a line on the back of the border fabric along the edge of the ruler.

5. Place a pin at the ¼" seam along the edge of the quilt top where you stopped sewing. Make sure it lines up with the seam directly behind it. Then place as many pins as necessary on the line you drew. If you have more than one border you will want a pin at every seam and possibly more in between. Sew on the line. I prefer to drop my needle down at the point where the seams meet, (where I placed the first pin). After the needle is inserted, remove the pin and lower the foot. Sew about 3 stitches, and then backstitch to secure the seam. Now sew to the outer raw edge. If the miter looks good, trim the excess fabric from the back. Trim to a ¼" seam allowance.

6. Press the seam open on the back and trim the little tails.

7. Enjoy your great looking mitered seam.

**P**lain &

**P**ieced

**B**orders

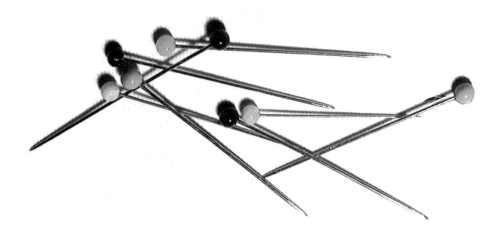

Let's take a quilt and look at different border options. Here is our sample quilt with no borders.

On the next 2 pages you will see twelve different border options for our sample quilt, but trust me, there are many more.

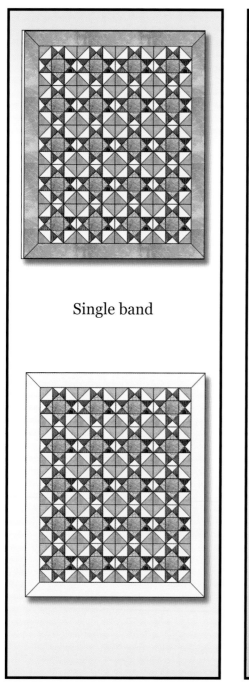

Single band

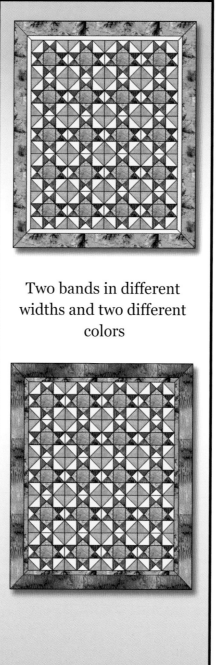

Two bands in different widths and two different colors

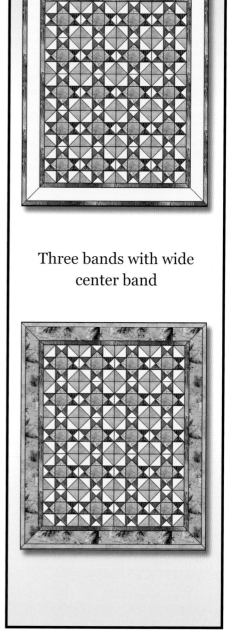

Three bands with wide center band

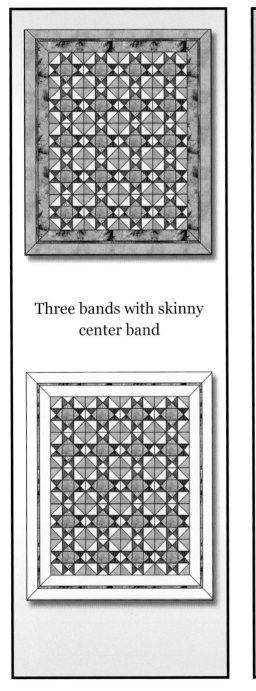

Three bands with skinny
center band

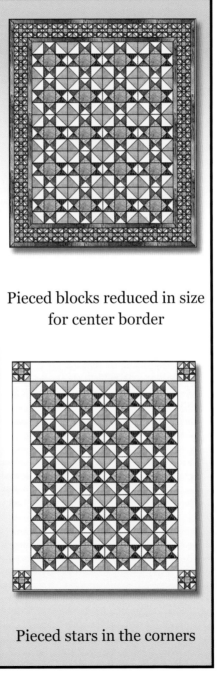

Pieced blocks reduced in size
for center border

Pieced stars in the corners

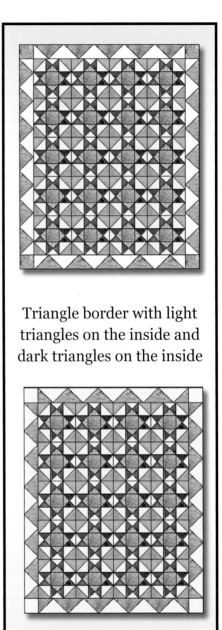

Triangle border with light
triangles on the inside and
dark triangles on the inside

# Working With Squares

If you have squares, 4-patch blocks or 9-patch blocks in the center of your quilt here are a few border ideas. The possibilities are endless.

a     b     c     d     e

a. single patch
b. 4-patch or sewn as strips
c. 9-patch or sewn as strips
d. alternating pieced block with solid block
e. combination of two blocks

Turning the corner on any of these designs would not be difficult.

 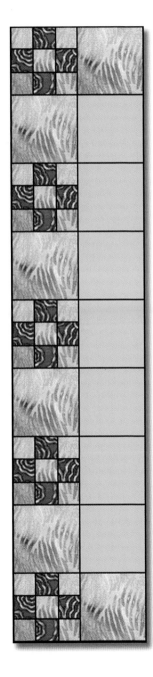 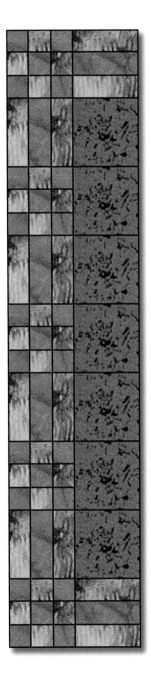

# Triangles and Getting Around the Corners

There are many quilt centers that will benefit from triangle units on the borders.

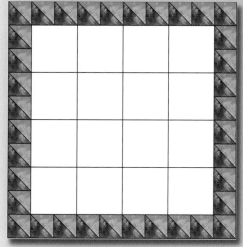

Triangles going in the same direction

Even number with change in center
Solid squares in corners

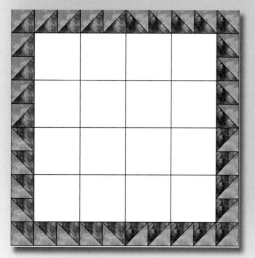

Even number with change in the center

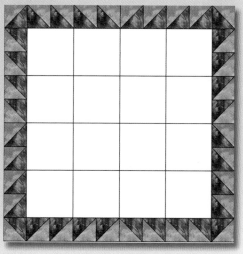

Even number with change in center

What else can you do with triangles?  The possibilities are endless.
Think outside the box.

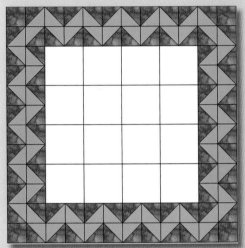

I love this layout
You could appliqué in the light area.

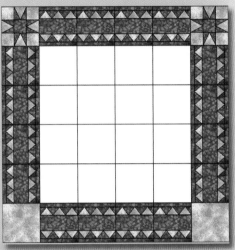

Two options for corners
You could appliqué in the center strip.

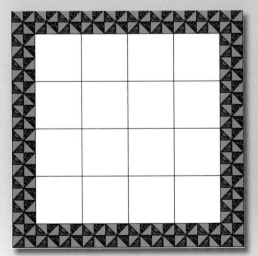

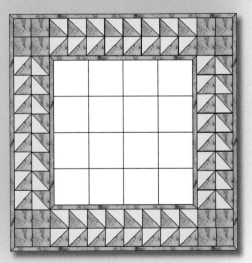

More good ways to play with triangles

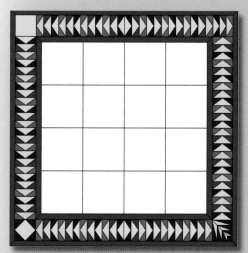

Four possible corner solutions
Side geese all going in one direction
Top and bottom geese change
direction in center

Taking a classic block like the Shoo-Fly
and placing it block to block can
create an interesting design

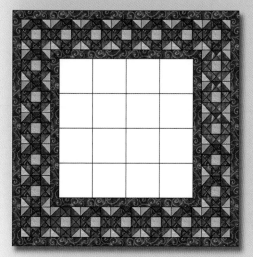

There are hundreds of star blocks
that would make excellent borders

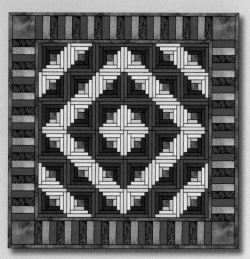

Using strips on the border since there
are strips in the center works well

There are lots and lots of blocks that form interesting designs when connected.

Fans

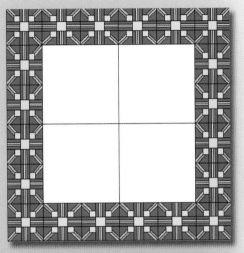

Diagonal block designs make very interesting borders.

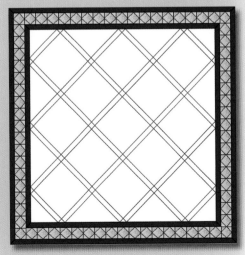

The Log Cabin
(One of my favorites)

A great option for an on-point layout is to use on-point blocks.

You can build the inner and outer border into the block (Three quilts on the previous page have separate strips for the inner and outer border.)

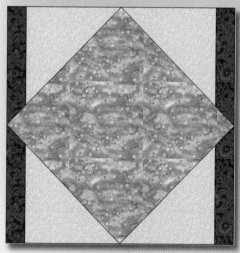

Side blocks

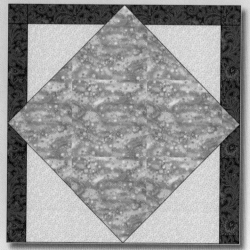

Corner blocks
(Could put strip on all 4 sides)

# Determining the Size of the Units/Blocks

Square quilts are the easiest, because the number of blocks is the same on all four sides.

If you are working on a rectangular quilt and your quilt measures 36" x 60", you want to look for a common denominator.

**Important**
Keep in mind the outside edge of any blocks used on the border needs to be on grain and not on the bias of the fabric. A bias edge makes it extremely difficult to attain a flat finished quilt. The bias has stretch and tends to distort the edge causing it to ripple.

Example A
> 36 divided by 3=12
> 60 divided by 3=20
> You would have 12 units on two sides and 20 units on the other two sides.
> Each unit would be a 3" square.

Example B
> 36 divided by 4=9
> 60 divided by 4=15
> Two sides would have 9 units and two sides would have 15 units.
> Each unit would be 4"

Which of these options would you choose? It would depend on the units/blocks you are planning to use on the border. Sometimes an even number of blocks is easier to work with to create new patterns in the border. For example, see the Log Cabin and Fan design on page 27.

If no number works there are several options. You could add a spacer border between the center portion of your quilt and the pieced border area. The spacer border could be a different width on the short and long sides. As long as they are close to the same size, it will not be noticed.   On a square quilt they would be the same.  Spacer borders often look good on any pieced border.  It is nice to have a break between the pieced center and the pieced border (A).

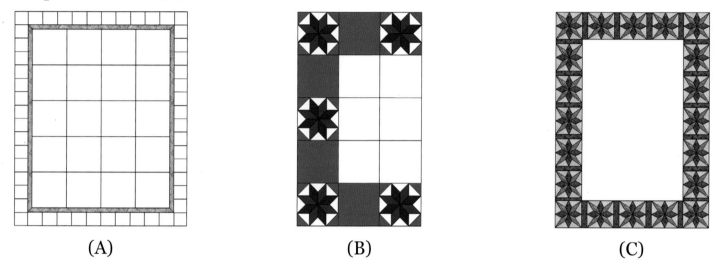

(A)                              (B)                              (C)

Other options would be to add strips (C) or solid blocks (B) between the units.

For a rectangular quilt try increasing or decreasing the size of the spacer strips by 1⁄4" at a time until you have a size that fits both borders.

If you know what size units you want, how do you determine how many you need?
If your quilt center measures 55" x 84" and you want to use 1 1⁄2" units.
55" divided by 1.5=36.666666
84" divided by 1.5=56 units/blocks
If you add a spacer border of 3 1⁄2" to the short sides, it would now be 58.5".
58.5" divided by 1.5 =39 units/blocks
If you add 3 1⁄2" to 84" it would measure 87.5" divided by 1.5=58.3333
But if you add just 3" to 84" it would measure 87".
87" divided by 1.5=58 units/blocks
Conclusion.  Make your spacer strips on the short sides 1 3⁄4" wide and your spacer strips on the long sides 1 1⁄2" wide.
If the spacer strips are cut from the same fabric, no one will notice the slight difference in width.

## Important

Always remember if you measure your quilt top from raw edge to raw edge you must subtract ½" for the seam allowances. You want to work with the finished size when calculating border sizes.

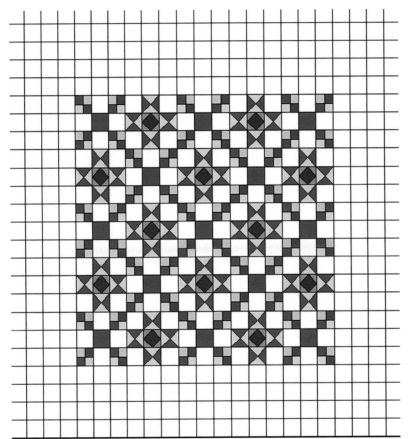

Drawing a sketch of the quilt on grid paper allows you to play with different border ideas. You could draw a different border on each side. It also allows you to try different corner ideas.

Working with colored pencils will allow you to experiment with color placement. Of course, there are many computer programs that allow you to do this with ease.

# Appliqué Borders

Appliqué borders can be simple or elaborate. They can add a graceful finish and make a smashing statement. Borders of this type are very effective when the center portion of the quilt is appliquéd, but they can also be a great finish to a pieced quilt. I love to appliqué which means I love to design and sew appliqué borders.

Whatever you decide to appliqué on your borders, do as much sewing on the strips as possible before you attach the borders onto the center area of the quilt. You will often have to complete some appliqué on the miters after the borders are attached.

As you are designing your appliqué border, always consider repeating elements from the center portion of your quilt. Sometimes you can repeat the exact size of the shape, and other times you many need to alter the size, but keep some shapes very similar to those in the center.

33

# Table Paper

Table paper is great for designing borders. It is the type of paper used on the examining table in your doctor's office. It is not expensive. It is thin so it folds accurately, and you can see through it. Since it comes on a roll, you can cut the paper as one piece, and do not have to tape several pieces together to get the length you need.

When working with table paper, begin by folding your paper in half. Then, fold the corner unit. This corner square will be the width of your border. Fold the remaining section in half. Keep folding the paper in half until you have your desired unit size. Folding your paper accordion style gives a more accurate result.

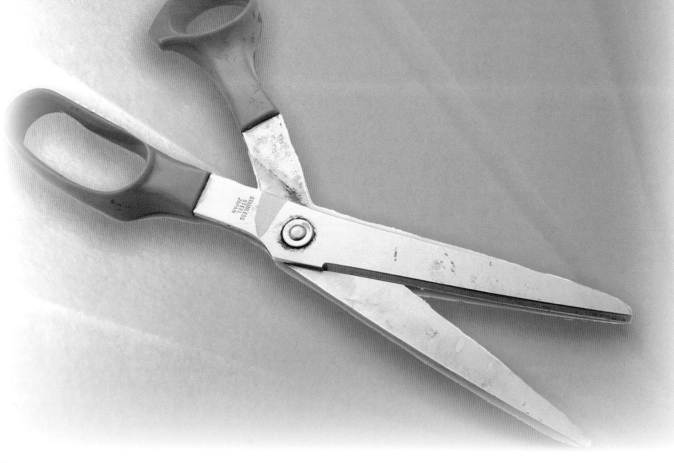

# Vines

**How do you get a continuous vine evenly spaced across the border?**

1. Start by cutting a piece of table paper the width and length of your border. (see page 36)

2. Fold the corner unit back. The corner unit will be the width of your border. If your border is 5" wide, fold back a 5" square. If your border is 3" wide, fold back a 3" square.

3. Now fold the remaining section of paper in half, then in half again, until you have it folded to a workable size.

4. Draw a curve on one folded section of paper. I often find that I like the curve to be a mirror image on the other side of the unit. So before you draw your curve, fold your unit in half. Start the curved line on the center crease, and draw to the center fold. Don't draw the curve to the outside edge of the paper. You need room to add flowers, leaves, grapes, etc.

I refer to this as the elliptical shape. Sometimes when you fold your paper and draw a curve, you could be working with a half circle shape rather than an elliptical shape.

# Vine exercise

1. Cut a piece of table paper or other thin paper 4¼" wide by 72" long.
2. Fold the length of your paper in half and crease the fold. You can draw a line on the crease but if you can see it well enough just crease the paper. Fold back a 4¼" square on each end.

4¼"                                                    4¼"

3. Fold your paper in half again and again.
4. Open the paper, and fold just one unit in half. With a pencil trace a curve in one half of the first unit. Start the curve on the center crease. If you don't like your curve, erase and draw again until you get a curve you like. French curves come in handy if you are having a bad day getting the right feel to the curve. French curves are easy to find at office supply stores. Trace this same curve on the other half of the first unit by folding the paper. If you have a hard time seeing your lines, place a piece of typing paper underneath. The white paper behind the table paper makes it easier to see the lines.

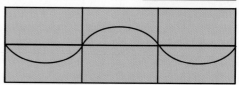

5. Make a template of your elliptical shape from template plastic. Flip the template up and down to complete the rest of the vine.
6. Add leaves, etc. to your vine. To make your own leaf pattern, fold a piece of paper and trace half of a leaf. Cut on the line you drew. When you open the paper, you will have a leaf that is equal on both sides. Make a template of the leaf from template plastic. Use this template to trace perfectly spaced leaves on your vine.

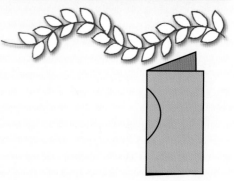

Drawing the elliptical shape on both sides of your center line will create a cable-vine.

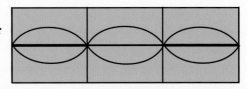

7. Design the corner units. There are many different ways to handle the corner. You could sew a pieced 4 ¼" square block pattern or an appliqué block for the corner unit. If you wanted to take the vine around the corner, what should you do?

   Fold the corner square on a 45-degree angle, or draw a line on the diagonal. Draw half of the design, and then trace the same design on the other half, creating a perfect mirror image.

   Here are a few ideas.

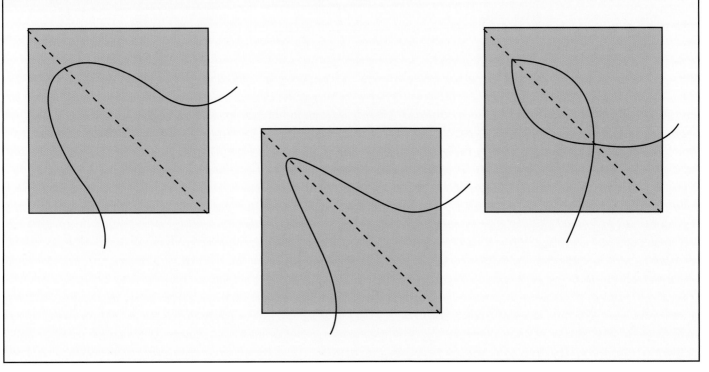

# Swag Border Design

1. Cut a piece of table paper the length of your quilt.
2. Fold the corner unit back (the width of your border).
3. Fold the remaining paper in equal sections.
4. Fold one unit in half to get a swag that mirror images on the other side.

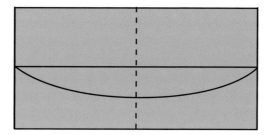

5. Before tracing the swags in every unit, draw half of a heart shape along the fold toward the center of the border.
6. You could make a template of the swag and heart, or simply trace the design onto the other sections by folding the table paper since the paper is easy to see through.

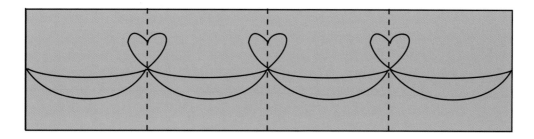

# Transferring the Design to Your Fabric

1. After you have your design traced in pencil on your table paper, retrace the lines using a fine tip Sharpie marker.
2. Place your paper pattern over a lightbox, glass door, window, etc. Center your cut fabric strip over the paper pattern.
3. Using the fabric marker of your choice, trace the design on to the right side of your border strip. I have been amazed that this method works on light as well as dark background fabrics.

# Appliqué Sawtooth Borders

The sawtooth border is based on half-square triangles. So your first step would be to determine your grid. The grid is the number of squares in the design. It is the number of equal divisions.

Let's draw a sample along the edge of a piece of typing paper.
1. Draw a line ½" from each short side of your paper. The distance between the lines is now 10". (The reason for decreasing the size is so we have an even number 1" grid. If you had an 11" edge on a quilt, you would want to add a spacer border so you would have an even grid.)
2. Draw a line ¼" from the long edge. This is your seam allowance.
3. Draw a horizontal line 1" from the ¼" line. Now draw a line every 1" on the vertical to create your 1" grid.
4. Draw a diagonal line through the center of each grid square following the pattern below.
5. Trace this design onto the paper side of a piece of freezer paper. Cut on the line. Make sure your freezer paper pattern includes the ¼" seam along the bottom edge.

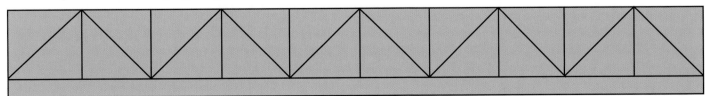

6. If the height/size of your unit is 1", cut your fabric strip 1" plus a ¼" seam allowance top and bottom. You should cut your  strip 1½", but I suggest cutting it a little larger just in case anything shifts. It gives you some room to play. Iron your freezer paper pattern onto the right side of a strip of fabric. The edge of the freezer paper will be on the raw edge of your fabric strip.

7. Trace along the edge of your freezer paper. This will be your sewing line.

8. Remove the freezer paper, and baste this strip of marked fabric to the right side of your base fabric/main border. You can thread baste or safety pin baste. (Keep your freezer paper pattern to use on the other three sides.) For more stability and better accuracy when you appliqué, cut the seam allowance and needleturn the edges as you go. If you trim the entire length of the strip all at one time, it will have too much give and may shift.

# Appliqué Steps

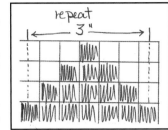

At first glance this border may look difficult. But after studying the step design you will soon find that it is based on a simple grid. The grid is the number of squares in the design. The grid used on my Buckley Album Quilt (see page 133) was a ½" grid. Each of my step sections were 3". A section is the area where it repeats.

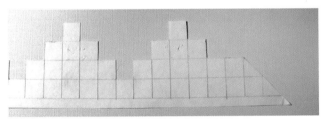

The other aspect to consider in designing the steps is the miter. In order to create a nice flow around the corners allow a 2" section on each end of your step strip. (Of course you could use a different grid size and you could have more or less steps. The choice is yours).

The method used to appliqué the steps is the same as the sawtooth method described on the previous pages. After you determine your grid and draw your step design, you need to make a freezer paper pattern. Remember to add a ¼" seam allowance along the bottom edge of your freezer paper strip. The freezer paper pattern will be ironed to the right side of your appliqué strip. Since my freezer paper pattern with the seam allowance on the bottom was 2 ¼ wide, I added a turn under allowance for my fabric and cut my fabric strip 2 ½" wide. Iron the freezer paper to the right side of the strip, and trace along the edge of the freezer paper. Remember to keep your freezer paper pattern to reuse on the other three sides.

Baste your marked strip to the right side of your main background fabric strip. The appliqué process is the same as with the sawtooth border. Cut a section, appliqué that section, then cut the next section and so on. To keep the steps even and smooth, it is best to cut and sew as you go.

# Other Perfect Finishes

43

# Piping

For several years I have been adding piping into many of my border seams. Including piping in the border gives some dimension. But the main benefit is to add a thin strip of color. I experimented with different thicknesses of cording on various projects. I will only use a thin cording on future projects. I had problems at the corners when I used thicker cording. It was also difficult to make the miters or straight seams smooth and even where the cording connects. I recommend a drapery cording 1/8" thick or thinner. I have worked with cotton and nylon cording. Be aware that cotton cording has shrinkage just like cotton fabric. It is a good idea to prewash and dry it before use to remove the shrinkage. Washing cotton cording in a lingerie bag works nicely.

You want your piping to contrast with the fabrics it touches. I often find that I want to bring a little of one color out from the center to help balance the colors in the overall project.

If you are undecided whether to add piping and/or the color of piping, cut a 1/8" strip of the fabric in the color you think will look good. Lay it along the seam where it might be placed. If you like the color, then proceed to make the piping. If not try another color.

# Making Piping

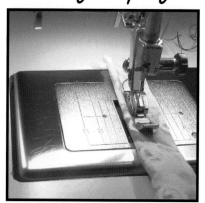

Cut a strip of fabric 1 1/2" wide on grain. Fold this strip of fabric in half. Lightly finger press a crease. Place the cording inside the crease. Place a zipper foot on your machine, and adjust the needle or foot as necessary. You will be sewing along this cording three times. Use a thread color that matches the cording fabric. (The samples are stitched in a contrasting thread color to allow you to better see the stitching.) The first two lines of stitching are slightly away from the cording. If you can adjust the needle position on your sewing machine, this step is very easy. Simply adjust it one position to the right of the edge of piping. If you do not have the option to move your needle position, simply shift your covered cording slightly to the left.

This strip needs to be trimmed to a 1⁄4" seam allowance. The 1⁄4" line of your ruler should be over the piping strip, along the right side of the cording, where you will be stitching when the border is added to the quilt top. Another easy and painless method for accurate trimming is to use Susan Cleveland's "Piping Hot Binding" tool (check your local shop or my web site).

Place this piece of covered cording on the right side/top of your cut border strip. Place the raw edges of the cording strip even with the border strip. Stitch on top of your previous line of stitching.

Place the piped border strip right sides together so the cording is in between the layers. The raw edges of your cording strip will be even with the raw edges of your quilt top. Sew as close to the edge of the piping as possible. This is your third and final line of stitching. Press the seam, and admire your beautiful piping.

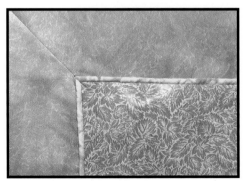

Follow the instructions for Mitering the Borders on page 16 and 17.

# Flange

After making several quilts with cording and sometimes having a difficult time in the miters I thought...what if there was no cording inside the fabric? I must tell you that I love this solution. It gives me the same look as when I was using cording, but it lies flatter and makes the joining of the seams very, very easy. It also gives a little dimension.

I test for color and design of the flange the same as I test for piping. I cut a ¼" strip of the fabric I think will work and place it along the seam where it will be sewn. Many times I have found that I like two flanges on the border seams. Sometimes I think I know which color will look good, and then, when I finish viewing my test strip I change my mind. It is far less time consuming to change your mind before it is sewn. It is just a matter of cutting another ¼" strip in another color and testing to see how a different color will look. It is a very minimal waste of fabric, and from the look of things in my house, there is no fabric shortage.

# Making the Flange

Cut a strip of fabric the length of your border by 1" wide. Press the strip in half, wrong sides together. The right side of the fabric should be facing you. Take your time pressing and be very accurate as this step will affect the evenness of the finished flange. Place the raw edges of your pressed strip even with the raw edges of your border strip. Sew with a little less than a ¼" seam allowance. Sew with a thread color that matches the flange. This is basically a basting stitch to hold the flange in place until you can sew it into the border seam.

For this example, the finished border will have two flanges. Sew one to the inner border strip and one to the outer border strip. Sew with a ¼" seam allowance. The raw edges of the flange will be even with the raw edges of the border strip.

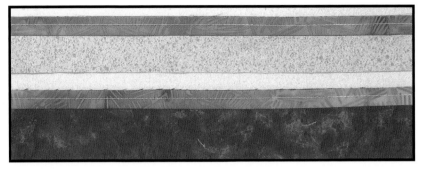

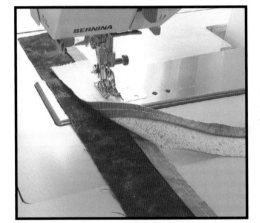

Place the inner and outer border strips right sides together with the flanges in the inside. Sew this seam.

Complete the miter as explained in Mitering the Borders on pages 16 and 17.

47

# Binding the Edge

Binding is the most common way to finish the edge. The binding covers the outside raw edges of your backing, batting and quilt top to create a smooth finished edge. Your quilting should be finished prior to adding the binding. If your project is going to get a lot of use, your fabric should be cut on the bias. The reason for using bias binding to finish an edge is that it has some give and will wear better. If your quilt will not get as much use, such as a wall quilt, then the binding fabric may be cut on grain.

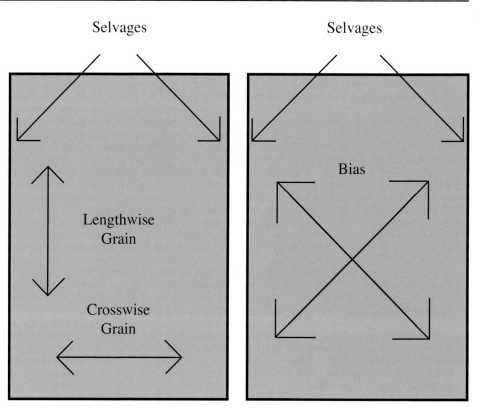

Fabric has a lengthwise grain, a crosswise grain and a bias. These grains are described in relationship to the selvages of the fabric. The selvages are the ends of the fabric where the threads are tightly woven to finish off the fabric edges. Crosswise grain runs from selvage to selvage. There is a little stretch on the crosswise grain. The lengthwise grain runs parallel to the selvages. There is little or no stretch on this grain of the fabric. Both crosswise and lengthwise grains are described as straight of grain. The bias of the fabric runs on the diagonal, a true 45 degrees to the crosswise and lengthwise grain and has the maximum amount of stretch.

# Straight Grain Binding

Cut strips of fabric on the grain 2" wide. Measure all four sides of your project, and add those four numbers together to determine how much binding you need. Then, add about 10" to that number to ensure you have enough fabric for seams, to get around the corners and to finish and connect the ends. Sew the strips together to make one long strip.

Join the strips with a diagonal seam. This reduces the bulk. In order to create a nice seam place two strips of fabric right sides together at a 90 degree angle. Draw a line from corner to corner.

Sew on the line and trim to a 1⁄4" seam allowance.

Press the seam open. You will now have one long strip of grain binding.

# Bias Binding

| | |
|---|---|
| 12" square yields | 55" |
| 18" square yields | 137" |
| 27" square yields | 326" |
| 36" square yields | 597" |

Bias binding is also easy to make. You must first determine how much fabric you need. To make bias binding you will start with a square piece of fabric. The chart shows you what size square you need in order to cut 2" wide strips of bias. It also shows how much it will make. I use 2" wide strips for my wall and bed quilts.

1. Cut a square piece of fabric the desired size. Fold the square in half matching the opposite corners, and press the fold. Cut on the pressed line so you now have two triangles exactly the same size.
2. Pin these two triangles right sides together as shown in Step 2. There should be a ¼" tip extending beyond each corner at this seam. Do not cut these tips away. Sew with a ¼" seam allowance. Press the seam open.
3. When you open the triangles, you will have a parallelogram. Use your ruler, and mark the entire back side of the fabric with lines spaced 2" apart and parallel to the bias. Cut into the first 2" line approximately 6".
4. Connect "X" to "O", forming a seam between "A" and "B". Use pins to line up the 2" lines at the seam. Sew this seam with a ¼" seam allowance. Continue to cut on the line where you made the 6" cut. When you are finished cutting, you will have one long continuous strip of bias binding.

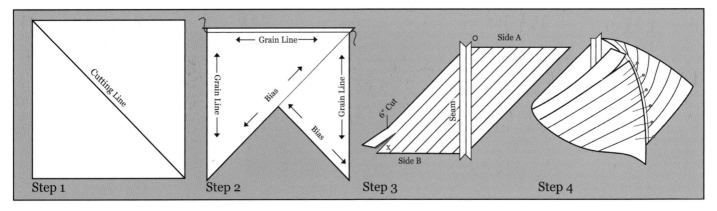

# Preparing to Attach the Binding

You can make either single fold binding, called regular binding, or double fold binding, often called French binding.

**Important**
Whether you make regular or double fold binding, cut your beginning tail (end of your strip) at a 45 degree angle.

The easiest way to make single fold binding is to run your fabric strip through a Clover Bias Maker. Feed the fabric strip, wrong side up, through the larger end of the bias maker starting with the 45 degree angle tail. There is a slit on the top of the bias maker. If your binding does not want to go through on its own, push it through with a pin. Place the bias maker on your ironing board, and iron the folds as they come out the small end of the bias maker. The bias maker folds the two sides over evenly. Keep your iron flat on the board and close to the end of the bias maker. If the iron is too far away from the end of the bias maker, you are more likely to have bumps instead of nice smooth edges. The bias maker does have a little handle to hold onto while you pull the fabric through.

 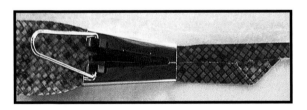

To make French binding, simply fold your 2" strip in half, wrong sides together and press.

# Attaching Binding With a Mitered Corner

Do not trim excess batting and backing until after you have stitched the binding.

For French binding:

1. Begin in the middle of a quilt side. Place your strip of fabric on the top of the quilt with the raw edges of the binding even with the raw edge of the quilt top. The folded edge will be facing in toward the quilt top. Leave about a 6" tail unstitched where you begin. On your sewing machine sew with a 1/4" seam allowance until you reach a corner. Stop sewing exactly 1/4" from the corner. Take a few backstitches, and remove the quilt from the sewing machine.
2. Fold the binding straight up as shown in the diagram at a 45 degree angle.
3. Fold the binding down so it is now even with the next side to be stitched. Place your quilt back in the sewing machine, and begin sewing 1/4" from the end. Backstitch and then sew with a 1/4" seam until you reach the next corner. Continue until all four corners are mitered in this same manner. Stop stitching about 8" away from the starting point.

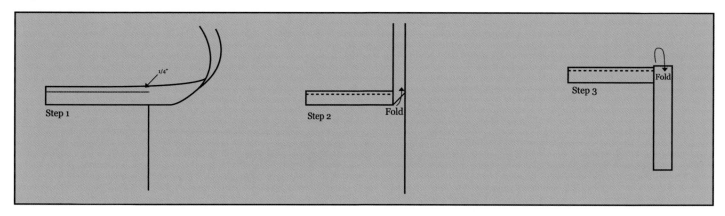

For regular binding:

Open one fold and place it right sides together along the raw edge of the quilt top. The other folded edge will be in toward the quilt top as you sew. Follow the steps for making French binding except sew in the fold and not on the 1/4".

After the binding is attached, trim the excess batting and backing.

# A Smooth Connection

Remember those tails at the beginning and end? Now you are going to connect them to create a smooth seam. As was suggested in the Preparing to Make the Binding section, your starting tail should be cut at a 45 degree angle. (The samples were stitched with two different fabrics so you can more easily see the connection.)

There should be an 8" to 10" space between where you started and stopped your stitching. The bottom tail should be cut so it lies flat within the 8" to 10" area. (The bottom tail can be cut with a straight edge or an angle cut.)

Open the folded fabric, and place the top tail over the bottom tail. Be sure they are lying down nice and flat. Draw a line where the two tails overlap on the 45 degree angle.

Draw a line 1/2" over from the line you just drew toward the raw edge. Cut on that line, and remove the excess fabric.

Pin the two ends with the right sides together. This creates little triangle tails that extend past the ends. Make sure there are equal amounts on both sides. Be careful at this step. The bias of the fabric has give, and you want to be cautious so it does not stretch.

Sew a ¼" seam in from the raw edge. Press the seam open.

Fold your strips back in, then place and lay them along the raw edge of your quilt top. Pin the strip in place. You are now ready to finish sewing your binding.

Fold your binding over to the back, and hand stitch the fold along the back side. Use a thread color that matches your binding to appliqué this fold.

## *Scallops*

Adding scallops takes a little time but is not difficult and well worth the effort. Consider adding the scallops when the quilting is almost complete. Quilting reduces the size of your quilt. The type of batting you use can also be a factor. Therefore, it is better to do most of the quilting and then take a measurement for the scallops. Stop quilting about 1" from the outside edge of your quilt. You need to have some space to insert the scallops and attach them to the edge.

Measure all four outside edges minus the seam allowance. Write each of the measurements on a piece of paper. These measurements should be close to the same size. If they are slightly different, it is not a problem to ease a little on one or two sides. Add these four measurements together, and divide by four. This will give you the average which is the length you will use on all four sides if you are making a square quilt. If you are making a rectangular quilt, you would take the average of the two short sides and then the average of the two long sides.

Table paper works great for this next step. Cut a piece of paper the size of your finished border/scallop area. You really need to be concerned with the length at this time. The width will be determined by how wide you want your scallop. If your finished scallop is only 3⁄4" high, you might want to cut your table paper 1 1⁄4" wide to give yourself a little space on the width to make adjustments.

After your paper is cut to the desired width and length, fold it in half. Then, fold in half again and again until you have it folded to a size you desire. If you are making a rectangular quilt you will need to cut two pieces of table paper. Cut one piece for the top and bottom border and one piece for the sides. When you do this folding step you want to try to get the sections folded as close to the same size as possible.

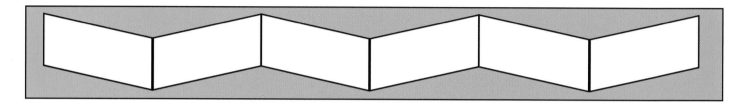

If I am adding a scallop, I like the size to relate to the curve or curves in the center. Having the curves on the border close to the same size as those in the center creates a balance to the overall quilt. When you have made the final fold, you can visually see the exact area you have to fill. Find something with a curved edge such as a plate, circle template, lid, or use a compass. For those of you who are mathematically inclined, I am certain you could divide the finished edge into equal sections. I tell everyone that my sister, who is a year older and was a math major, got all of the math brain cells. A year later when I came along, there were none left. Some of you will find the paper folding method easier, and some of you will find it easier to divide and conquer. The nice thing is that in the end we all get the same result.

After you have folded or mathematically calculated the area to be filled, draw the curve onto the first section. You also want to draw your 1/4" seam allowance.

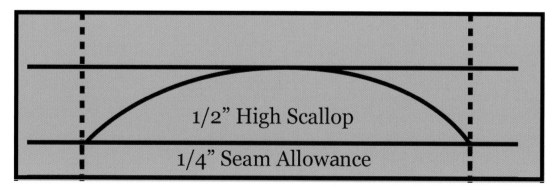

1/2" High Scallop

1/4" Seam Allowance

Mark the same curves in the remaining folds on your table paper. Tape your paper to the table. Next, cut a piece of freezer paper, and place it over your table paper. Begin by drawing a line ¼" from the straight edge of your freezer paper for your seam allowance. You do want the seam allowance marked on this paper. Trace the exact lines and curves from your table paper onto your freezer paper. Tip: To save some marking and cutting time, trace half of the design and fold the freezer paper in half. Staple inside the curved area. Then cut along the curve. Remove the staples with your staple remover, and open the pattern to its full size.

Cut your scallop fabric a little longer and wider than your freezer paper pattern. Iron the freezer paper pattern to the back side of one fabric strip. Make sure the straight edge of the freezer paper is lined up with the straight edge of the fabric. Trace along the curved edge of the paper with the fabric marker of your choice. Repeat on the back of three more strips. You will need a total of four strips marked to complete the border.

Place one marked strip with right sides together with an unmarked strip. Cut a strip of batiste the same size as your border. (Batiste is a light weight fabric and makes a great interfacing. It is often used by garment sewers.) The batiste will end up inside the scallop adding more stability. (You could use other types of stabilizers or possibly some batting in this step.) Place the batiste behind the unmarked strip. Pin these three layers together. With a slightly smaller stitch size, sew on the line you drew for the curves. I usually sew with about 12 stitches to the inch, but for this I stitched about 16 stitches per inch. It is really important to sew on the curved lines to keep your finished scallops smooth. Make it easy on yourself to stay on the line by using an open embroidery foot, a clear plastic foot, or a foot that has a line marked down the center. As you reach the inner point, take one straight stitch across, then pivot, and stitch into the next curve. This one stitch will create a sharper inner point when this is trimmed and turned inside out.

With a pair of pinking shears, trim around the curved edge. This will reduce the bulk and give you a smoother curve. Then, take one clip straight into each inner point just shy of your sewing line.

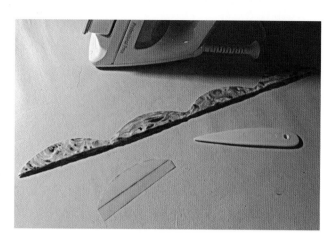

Turn your sewn and trimmed strip inside out. Push the curve open using a point turner. From Templar or other brand of heat resistant plastic make a template of just one of your curves with about ½" seam allowance added to the straight edge. (Templar is a heat resistant plastic which is needed for this step as it will be used with an iron.) This added seam allowance gives you something to hold onto. Push this template inside the curve, and press the edge. Trim to ¼" seam from the raw edge.

If you have not already done so, trim your batting and backing even with your quilt top. Trim a ¼" of batting away from the outside edge. To trim the batting, slide your rotary mat board between the batting and backing. Place a ruler along the edge of the batting and with your rotary cutter trim the batting. Do this on all four sides. The reason for trimming the batting is to open an area for the seams of the scallop. If you do not trim the batting the seams along the outside edge will be too thick and bulky.

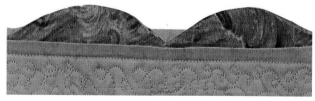

Place the raw edges of your scalloped border even with the raw edges of your quilt top. Sew a ¼" seam allowance.

Flip the scalloped border out. With your walking foot, quilt ¼" from the edge.

Fold a ¼" seam down on the backing fabric. Pin this edge even with the scallop and hand appliqué.

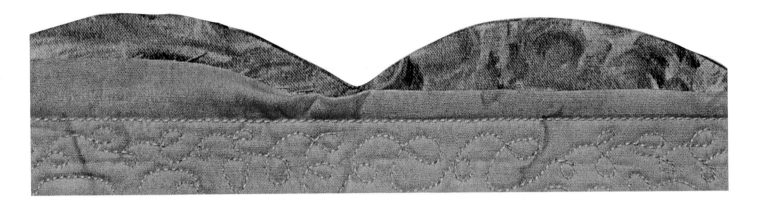

# Karen's Top Ten Tips and Tricks for Piecing and Appliqué

## Tips for accurate piecing.

1. Make sure you are sewing with an accurate ¼" seam allowance. Sew some accurately cut scraps together before sewing the entire quilt top. For example, if using 2 ½" squares for a quilt top take two of those squares and sew them together. After they are joined, open the unit and press the seams to one side. They should measure 4 ½". If they do not, make the necessary adjustments.

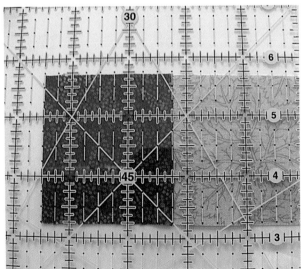

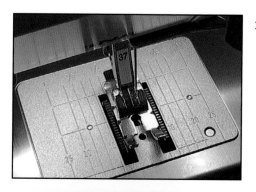

2. To aid in attaining a perfect ¼" seam allowance use a ¼"patchwork foot on your sewing machine. Most sewing machine manufacturers make this specialty foot just for your machine.

3. Even when using a ¼" patchwork foot I also like to use a guide along the edge of my sewing machine foot. Having a guide makes the sewing mindless and accurate. There are different metal guides made by many sewing machine manufacturers or you could cut and use a strip of molefoam along the edge of your foot. Be sure to keep the molefoam away from your feed dogs.

4. Using a straight stitch throat plate on your sewing machine helps to keep the fabric tails from being eaten by your sewing machine. It is also a very important accessory when machine quilting. It helps with your stitch tension and creates a more even stitch.

5. Proper maintenance of your machine is a must for good piecing. It is recommended to sew with a needle for only about ten hours. After that, the point becomes dull and may damage the fabric as it pierces through the layers. Check your sewing machine manual for the areas to oil and how frequently you should oil your machine. Treat your machine well and it will treat you well.

## Tips for smooth curves and sharp points on your appliqué shapes.

6. To create sharp points on your appliqué shapes follow these directions. Trace a leaf shape onto a piece of Templar or heat resistant plastic using a pencil. Cut the shape using your paper scissors. If the edges are not smooth file them with an emery board. Position the Templar shape on the back of the fabric and trace around the edge. Cut outside the line you drew adding a little less than ¼" seam  allowance. Place the fabric shape face down on your pressing board. Paint the seam allowance with Magic Sizing. Using the side of your iron push the seam up and over the edge of your Templar. Do one side, then the other side. There will be some excess at the points.

Hold the seams where they cross. Paint the tip with sizing. Take the excess and fold or pleat it in toward the back. Press with the iron until dry.

The points will look really sharp. When you are satisfied with the edge, remove the Templar and appliqué your shape in place.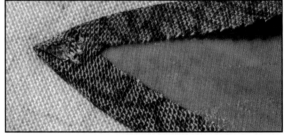

7. I love it when people look at my appliqué edges and cannot see the thread I used. For hand appliqué I have found that a fine, thin thread makes all the difference. I prefer a 60/2 cotton thread. Some sewers prefer silk thread. The bottom line is to use a fine, thin thread so your stitches are hidden. For machine appliqué, I prefer my edges to be turned under, and I use a thin clear nylon or monofilament thread on the top of my machine as well as in the bobbin. This combination has never caused any damage to the machine. It sews beautifully.

8. How you stitch the points, both inner and outer, on your hand appliqué makes a big difference. On outer points take just one stitch that is slightly longer. It picks up slightly more background fabric than normal stitching. This one straight stitch out from the point makes your points look sharper, but it is really that single strand of thread coming off from the point that fools the eye.

For hand appliqué the inner points can be a very weak spot as no seam allowance is turned under in this area. When you reach the inner point take three tack stitches about two to three threads into the fabric. I used to stack those stitches on top of each other but then found I got a better result if I fanned the stitches out. I take one stitch to the left, one in the center and one to the right. As I sew these three tack stitches I only catch the appliqué fabric and not the fabric under my appliqué shape. It allows the threads to cinch closed and creates a better inner point. Try it sometime.

9. Needles are another important part of the process. For machine sewing my favorite needle is a Microtex/Sharp. And I really love the 60/8 size. It makes a very fine hole in the fabric, and the thread fills the small hole giving me a nice clean finished edge.

For hand appliqué the needle I prefer is a John James sharp in a size 10. However, I really think it is wise to test different needles when it comes to hand appliqué. There are lots of choices on the market. You may find something that feels more comfortable in your hand, and allows you to get a better stitch. I'm always testing new needles as they come on the market in case I find something that allows me to make a better stitch.

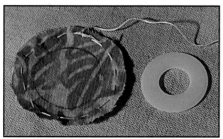

10. My top appliqué tip is making perfect circles. I have a product called "Perfect Circles™", and this is how it works. Trace around the circle on the wrong side of your fabric. Cut the circle adding a 1/4" seam allowance. The exception is with smaller circles where a narrower seam allowance is needed.

With knotted thread, sew a running stitch midway through the seam allowance. Place the fabric circle on your pressing cloth right side down. Place the circle in the center of the fabric circle.

Pull on the thread, and the seam will gather around the circle. To keep the seam snug, hold tightly, and pull the thread across the circle. Spray some Magic Sizing into the lid of the container. It comes out foamy but within a few seconds it will become liquid.

While holding the thread, use a small stencil brush or a Q-tip, and paint the seam allowance with Magic Sizing. Place a dry, hot iron onto the back of the circle. The iron will need to remain on the fabric long enough for the sizing to dry. This takes a little time because the sizing soaks into the gathers. As this circle is drying under the iron, start a running stitch in the seam allowance of the next circle. The timing is perfect. By the time you finish sewing on the second circle, the first circle is dry. It is a little assembly line process. After the sizing is dry, loosen the seam where you finished your running stitch. The end of the running stitch is easy to find if you left a tail of thread.

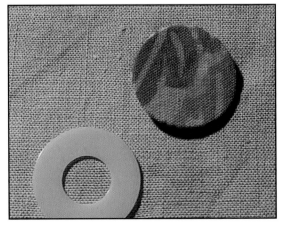

After removing the circle, pull again to close the seam. You now have a perfect circle to hand or machine appliqué on your favorite project. You can find these for sale at many local quilt shops or through my web site **www.karenkaybuckley.com**.

# Conclusion

After reading the information on the previous pages and viewing the quilts in the gallery, I hope you will consider trying something different on your next quilt border. My goal has been to try something different with each new quilt.

After each project is finished I encourage you to sign your quilt. Place a label on the back of each quilt with your name, the date the quilt was finished, and the name of the quilt. When I first started to quilt my instructor recommended including the number of the quilt on each label. In other words, if I was just finishing my 12th quilt I would include the #12 on the label. When my instructor talked about doing this I was sewing on my first quilt. I could not imagine that I was going to make that many more quilts so I never numbered my labels. Today I wish I had followed her advice.

This is the raffle quilt for the Letort Quilte
2000. Janet and I designed the top, select
the fabric and washed and ironed the fabri
Several of us got together to assemble the
kits which were distributed to members in
Spring. The top was together in the sumn
and Kitty Henry started quilting the end of
The quilt was finished in the Winter of 20
It is a fabulous quilt. Hand appliquéd and
quilted.
Made: 1999-2000
Design: Star of Hope

I wanted to play with this pattern by doing paper piecing on the straight edges and machine appliqué on the curves. (I hate piecing curves.) It went really well. I machine quilted it one day during the girls trip at the beach. The yellow strips around the border were made with folded fabric.
Made: Summer 1999
Design: Ocean Sunrise

I have, however, documented my progress in a different way.

I keep journals which include every quilt I have ever made. On the pages in my journals I include the time period in which the project was sewn, a story or information about why the quilt was made or what inspired me to make that quilt. I also include swatches of every fabric used in the quilt and a photograph of the project. I encourage you to do the same.

# Gallery

All the quilts in this gallery are the work of the author. Every effort was given to credit any sources that aided in the designs. I apologize if any sources were missed.

# Dreaming of the Tropics 80"x 80"

*Hand appliquéd and hand quilted*

**T**his was my first appliqué medallion style quilt. It was inspired by a 1500's Italian mosaic. I found that I really loved the balance of medallion style quilts and have continued to make many more. This quilt changed the way I approached my projects. I did something on this quilt that I had never done before but have since incorporated into my work. I traced the design on my black background as with most of my other work. But then, I cut every piece of appliqué fabric and placed it on the black background fabric in its traced location to determine if I liked the color. If I did not like the color or there was too much of that color, I pulled those pieces down and tried something else. This method is now standard with my design and color process. I found that it was easy to change my mind before the appliqué was complete. Let's face it, after all the work of appliquéing, you might decide your choice of color doesn't look all that bad. You are more apt to change it before it is appliquéd.

After completing the appliqué in the center, I could not decide on a border design that would enhance the center. All of a sudden I realized I loved the quilt just the way it was and made the decision not to add a border. A decision I have never regretted.

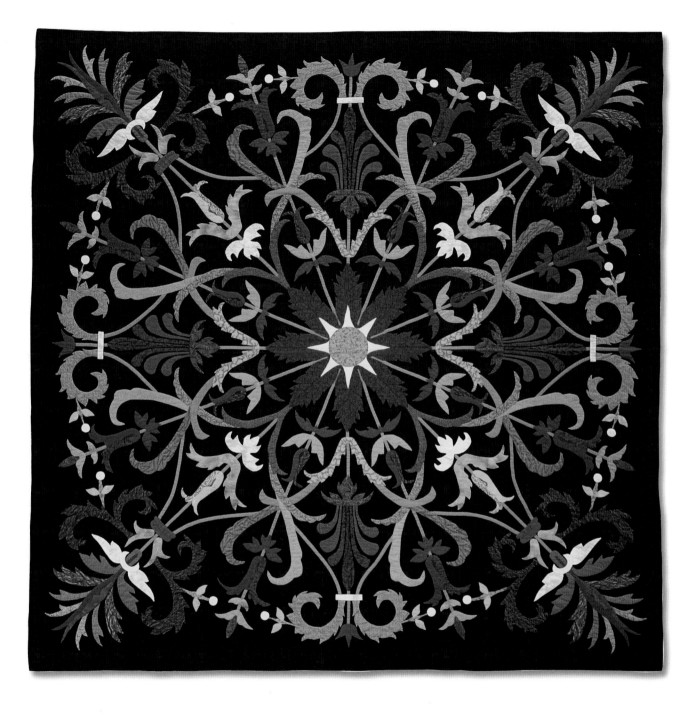

# Country Time 82" x 78"

*Hand appliquéd, fabric paint, machine embroidered and machine quilted*

Working from several photographs I had taken over the years, I created my version of the perfect summer scene.

I could not find fabric to suit the style of leaves I needed for some of the plants so I painted fabric to achieve the look I wanted. I was very satisfied with the outcome and would not hesitate to add paint again. I considered adding a single band of fabric around the outside edge but knew that was not the look I desired. In one of my mail order catalogs I found an oil painting in which the artist painted a single brush stroke an inch or two in from the edge. I liked this approach and adapted it to my quilt. But instead of painting my strip, I braided three strips of fabric and then appliquéd them around the edge. I loved this finish and would use it again.

# Folk Art Fantasy 37" x 21"

*Hand appliquéd and machine quilted*

I was walking through an antique show and noticed this wonderful painting on the side of an old chest. I asked the owner if I could sketch and photograph the design and she said, "Yes." When I got home I could hardly wait to start drawing the design and make fabric selections. I am very grateful to the antique dealer for allowing me to use the design. This quilt has the feeling of Pennsylvania Dutch designs which remind me of home.

When I reached the edge I wanted the viewer to know they were at the edge without the use of a border. I decided to appliqué a strip of fabric 1 1/2" in from each side. I am very satisfied with the results.

# Hexagonal Beauty 61" x 57"

*Machine pieced by author, and hand quilted by Helen Heckert*

Three of my girlfriends joined me on a fabric shopping trip and we saw this wonderful antique quilt in a little shop. When I got back into the car my girlfriend, Lytle, and I were both sketching. I asked her what she was sketching. We were both sketching the same quilt pattern. When we returned home we developed a way to strip piece the project and had lots of fun doing it. The center portion of this quilt is busy from using a lot of different fabrics. A single band of a dark fabric on the outside edge creates a great frame and a place to rest your eyes.

# Garden Medley 21" x 24"

*Hand appliquéd and machine quilted*

One day I was sketching some ideas for a hand appliqué class. After completing the center panel I decided I liked the project so much I designed two more panels. The simplicity of just placing the lattice around the outside edges was a perfect finish to this little project.

# Bears, Bears, Bears 38"x 60"

## *Hand appliquéd and machine quilted*

When my sister was pregnant with her second child she selected a beautiful wallpaper border for the new baby's room. The wallpaper inspired me to create this quilt with Bear Paw blocks and appliqué bears. My husband, Joe, helped me design the bears.

Repeating the same light fabric from the center of the quilt on the border gave the quilt a more open feel. I tend to like a dark finish on the edge so I decided to sew strips of all the darker fabrics used in the center to create this rainbow binding.

77

# Flowers and Friends II 53" x 53"

*Hand appliquéd and hand quilted.  Quilting by Sandy Chambers*

fter making Flower and Friends I, I decided to make several of the blocks for this smaller quilt on a darker background.  I was always glad I made this before I wrote my book, "Appliqué Basics: Flower Wreaths", which includes all of the patterns from this quilt plus those from Flower and Friends I.  I ran into some interesting tribulations going from the light to the dark background.  All were solvable and are explained in the book.  Just to give you one idea,  on my light background fabric I drew the grape vine squiggles using a permanent fabric marker.  When I worked on the dark background I had to embroider the grape vine squiggles. If I had drawn them on with a dark permanent fabric marker no one would have been able to see them.

As I was sewing these blocks, I was thinking about the border and my first instinct was to place a swag border around the outside edge.  After I cut the table paper to the size of my border I looked right in front of me and on the table were all the templates I had used for the blocks in the center of the quilt. I started to draw a random vine and then picked up the templates and traced around them.  If you look closely you will notice that all of the shapes from the butterfly block are grouped in one section of the border.  Then, all of the shapes from the tulip block are grouped into another section, and so on.  I sectioned the border in five, not so even, sections.  As soon as I was done drawing this border I knew I would never draw a swag border as I loved this one too much.  It brings all the elements and colors from the center to the outside frame creating a beautiful balance.

# Dimensionality I 75"x 49"

*Machine pieced, machine appliquéd, machine embroidered and machine quilted*

**W**ow! This was a fun quilt to make. My quilt guild, the Letort Quilters, holds a challenge for their members every two years. One year the challenge was to make a quilt related to opposites, and it had to be embellished using something with a hole. I made a single block which I call "The Kiss". It was inspired by a Victor Vasarely design. Many guild members commented on the block when it was displayed in the challenge and that prompted me to see if I could use that block in a larger project. I challenged myself to make a black and white quilt, along with grays. One thing led to another, and soon I was experimenting with my sewing machine. The result was an avaunt-garde sampler quilt. Because the center portion was fairly elaborate, a single band of black fabric around the outside seemed the perfect solution, with a few tassels and triangles thrown in.

# Trip Around the Flower Garden 31" x 31"

*Hand appliquéd and machine quilted*

I enjoy combining appliqué with piecing. Some of my favorite quilts combine these two elements. I based this center design on an antique quilt block and then, added Trip Around the World corner blocks. Using the same fabric for the border as the outer triangles allows the design to bleed into the border making it appear as one piece instead of triangles with a single strip of fabric around the outside.

# Applesauce 37"x 31"

*Machine pieced and machine quilted*

This pattern is sometimes called Apple Core, Spools, or Double Ax. When I was growing up we had a large apple tree in our backyard and using those apples my mother made the world's best applesauce. My mom's applesauce is one of my favorite foods. No one makes it better. (My neighbor, Mr. Howe, comes in second.) I had to name my quilt after one of my favorite foods. Many times the design elements in the center can simply be carried through to the border. When this quilt was assembled, the black units were stitched into the rows. Row one was all black units. Row two was a black unit connected onto each end and then joined to row one and so on.

After I painstakingly made sure all of the intersections where the units met were perfect, I covered them up with yarn. Had I known I was going to add the yarn I would never had taken so much time restitching intersections to make them all perfect. The black yarn was left over from my knitting days and was couched over every seam. The couching was completed after all of the layers were together so the couching also became the quilting.

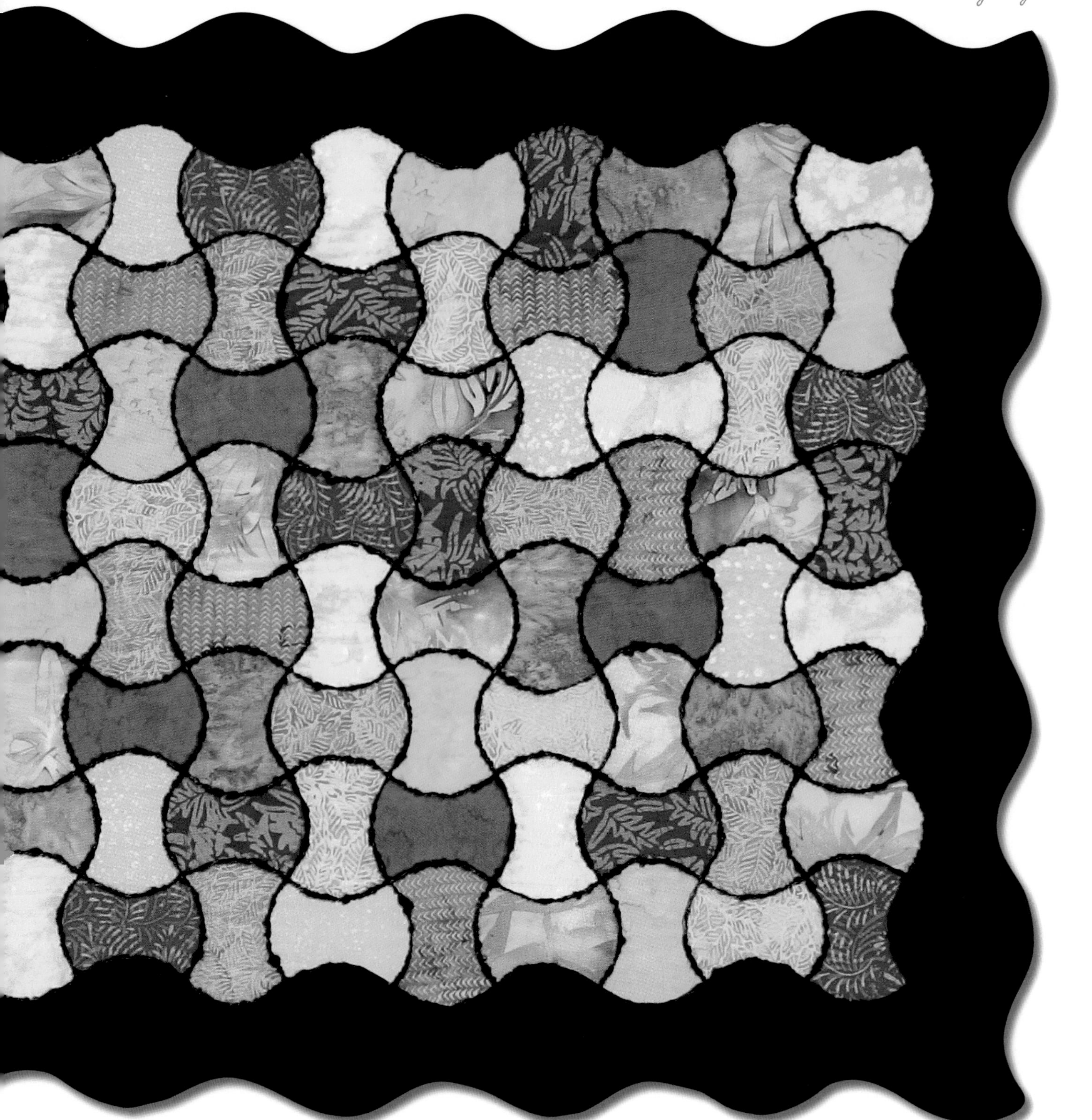

# Ocean Sunrise 48" x 48"

*Machine pieced, machine appliquéd and machine quilted*

I have always loved this block design. When paper piecing became popular I decided this was a project I could do. However, I am not in love with piecing curved seams so I machine appliquéd my curves. Sewing the curves using machine appliqué made me very happy. I had a difficult time deciding what to do on this border. I tried adding some pieced blocks to the border but did not like the way it looked. What I needed to do was keep it simple. I was going to use just a single band of navy blue fabric, but that seemed bland. So I cut some 1/4" strips of yellow fabric and placed them along the sides of the single band of navy blue. As soon as I saw them on the design board I knew adding the two yellow flanges to the seams was just what this quilt needed.

# Magical Medallions 84" x 84"

*Hand appliquéd and machine quilted*

There is something about the symmetry of the medallion style that is very appealing to me. After making numerous medallion style quilts and being asked if I could teach my methods, I decided to design this project. Each square uses the same techniques as my larger medallion quilts and allows me to teach all of my techniques on these smaller blocks rather than an 80" block. After I finished all of the blocks I wanted to incorporate curves on the outside edge. A friend and fellow quilter, Sue Nickels, suggested adding scallops. Scallops on the border are the perfect complement to the curves around the frame of each block. I first placed a single strip of fabric around the project before adding the scallops. In order to keep a nice balance to the quilt, the scallops were made close to the size of the curves in the center.

# Magical Medallions 44" x 44"

*Hand appliqué and machine quilted*

After making Magical Medallions (Tan) I decided to take four of the blocks from that project and make this wall quilt. It was difficult to select just four blocks because I loved all of the blocks in the previous quilt. But I was finally able to make the selection. I considered making this project from the same fabrics as the larger version, however, I find it difficult to repeat the same fabrics when I have so many incredible choices. Again I knew connecting scallops to the single band of fabric on the border would be a great way to finish the edge.

# Opulent Ornaments 29" x 29"

*Machine pieced, machine embellished and machine quilted*

To make this quilt I first traced the outline of an ornament shape on a piece of muslin. I then crazy patch pieced on the muslin until the ornament area was filled. Next, I placed a piece of fabric over the top and cut the ornament shape away so the crazy patching would show through the opening. Crazy patching on the corners was fun. It allowed me to experiment with a lot of decorative stitches on my sewing machine that I had never used. It also allowed me to top stitch several types of trims to the seams to give the quilt more of a Victorian feel. I tried a single band of fabric around the outer edges to see if I liked it, but something was missing. I decided to make a smaller version of the ornament and placed it in the corners pulling everything together and unifying this little wall quilt.

# Plaids in the Pines 51 x 38"

*Machine pieced and machine quilted*

I really liked the pine tree block and thought it could add to my Christmas décor. The blocks were fun and easy to make. I enjoyed playing with my collection of green plaid fabrics to make every tree. I actually had enough different green plaid fabrics that I could make every tree from a different fabric. As I approached the border a single band of fabric just seemed like it was not enough. When I added the strip of lattice fabric on the border it all seemed to work. This wonderful little quilt hangs inside my door every year during the holidays.

# Geese in Flight 60" x 60"

*Paper pieced and machine quilted*

After receiving a copy of McCall's Quilting magazine I saw this fabulous quilt designed by Cindi Edgerton. Her quilt used graduated colors of hand dyed fabrics. I had some stunning packets of hand dyed fabrics in my collection. I had purchased them just because I liked the colors. I had no idea when I bought them what I would do with them. I thought this would be an excellent project in which to use them. When I reached the border I knew I wanted just a splash of the purple color I had used in the center of my blocks so I added a piping in the seams of the border. This was one of the projects I mentioned in the section on piping. I used a cording that was about 3/4" of an inch thick which made it difficult when I got to the miters. I like the idea of the piping, but if I had this project to do again I would have selected a thinner cording.

# Vegetable Garden 40"x 30"

*Machine appliquéd, machine pieced and machine quilted*

For our guild's 12<sup>th</sup> anniversary they challenged each member to make a project that reminded us of when we were 12 years old. One of the memories I have is picking vegetables and weeds from the family garden. Notice my quilt just has the vegetables. Since pulling weeds was not one of the better memories, I did not put any in my quilt. The idea for this project came from the front of seed packets. I remember looking at the packets when I was a young girl and how amazed I was that a little seed could grow into something so large. Originally, I was going to design just three blocks. After three blocks were completed I liked them and thought...maybe four blocks would be nice. After the fifth block I had to make six to balance the design. I swear I could have made this quilt really large if the deadline for the challenge was not fast approaching.

The combination of three bands of fabric with the center band being a wider strip is always pleasing to my eye. By repeating the lattice fabric as the thinner border strips I was able to maintain a nice balance.

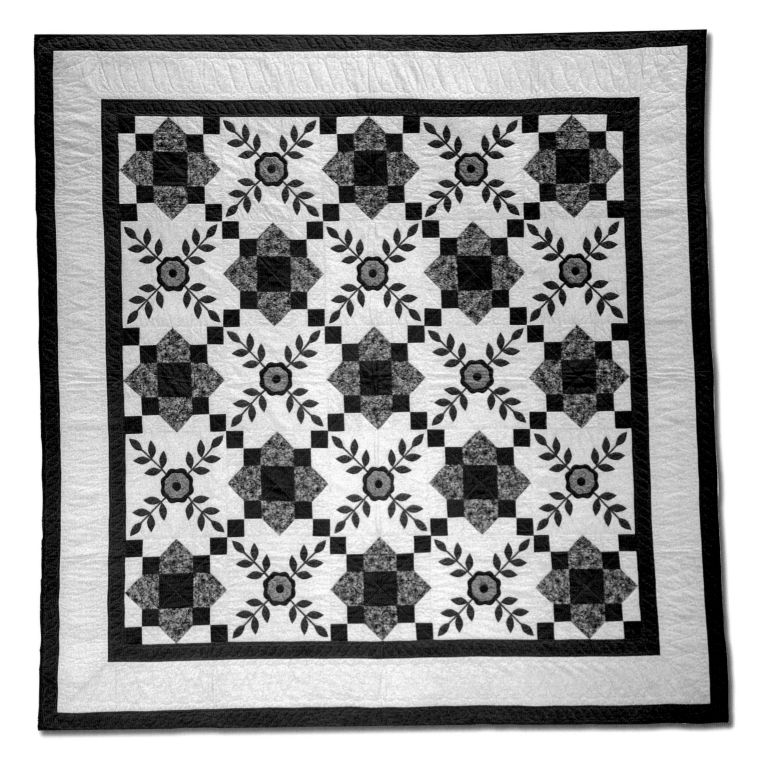

# Down the Garden Path 76" x 76"

*Machine appliquéd and machine pieced. Hand quilted by Helen Heckert*

I often find myself wanting to sew a traditional style quilt after doing a not so traditional quilt. That was the case with this quilt. I was in the mood to make a traditional quilt but using machine appliqué instead of hand appliqué. I like the diagonal flow of the quilt created from both the pieced and the appliquéd blocks. When I reached the border I wanted a simple frame and also a nice space for my quilter to play. Helen did a wonderful job hand quilting this project.

# Scrap Happy 64" x 64"

*Machine pieced and machine quilted*

My quilt guild asked me to design a project for our annual retreat weekend. They wanted it to be fun and easy. When I received this request I was in the process of collecting some of the incredible plaid fabrics that had just hit the market. I figured that my guild members could simply use light and dark scraps of fabrics from their stash piles. It would allow them to get rid of some scraps and make room for new fabric. However, when they saw my project I think 80% of them went out and purchased plaid fabrics for their projects. So in the end their stash piles were increased instead of decreased. (Not necessarily a bad thing.) When I was nearly finished sewing the center blocks together, I noticed that I had a lot of extra squares. I wondered if there was a way I could incorporate those squares into the border. I knew I would need a spacer strip in between the center portion of the quilt and the pieced squares, but knew it would bring unity to the quilt.

# Antique 9-Patch 23"x 23"

*Machine pieced and machine quilted*

**M**y husband, Joe, found these fabulous antique 9-Patch blocks at a flea market. When he brought them home I thought they would look nice all sewn together. What I came to realize was that all the blocks were different sizes and would never fit side-by-side. I put them in a box and forgot about them. Then, one day I was working on new projects for an advanced machine quilting workshop. I went searching for the blocks with this idea in mind. If I placed a single solid block between the 9-patch blocks and trimmed the 9-patch blocks all to the same size everything would fit.

On another excursion to the flea market Joe found the dark brown fabric used for the skinny middle border. I liked the idea of repeating the beige background fabric for the two wider strips and then coming down the center with a skinny strip of the antique brown fabric. I love this little quilt and it hangs in my office so I get to look at it every single day. Life is good.

# Pineapple Log Cabin 61" x 61"

*Machine pieced and hand quilted*

I have loved pineapple log cabin blocks for as long as I can remember. I wanted to make a pineapple log cabin quilt but never liked any of the directions for making one until I saw a pattern by Susan Bartlett. Susan had a pattern business called The Quilted Cottage. I worked from many of Susan's patterns over the years because they were easy to understand. I knew if Susan wrote directions on how to make this block that I could do it. I jumped in and started cutting strips. I had a system set up so I could sew a strip, walk to my right and press the strip. I then walked across the front of my table and picked up the next strip and back to the machine. I was dizzy from walking in a circle! But oh was I having fun. Now you have to understand that this occurred during the time I owned a quilt shop. Sewing time for me was scarce since the shop was so busy. But in the evenings I was walking in circles and loving it. One Friday afternoon when I was in my quilt shop my husband showed up at the shop. I was shocked. I thought maybe he quit his job or got fired. He never came into the shop during the week. He said everything was great. He decided to take the afternoon off and take care of the shop for me so I could go home and sew. I love Joe. He is the most thoughtful person I know. I practically ran out the door to go home and walk in circles.

As I was sewing the blocks I had this fabric in mind that I wanted to use for the border. I was going to use just a single strip of fabric for this border. I cut two strips and placed them along the edge of the quilt and I hated it. The print in the fabric was way too busy against an already busy center. I regrouped and found a solid brown fabric in my stash. Then, I found a green striped fabric and decided to add it to the mix. I loved the way this quilt finished. More than ten years later it is still one of my favorite quilts.

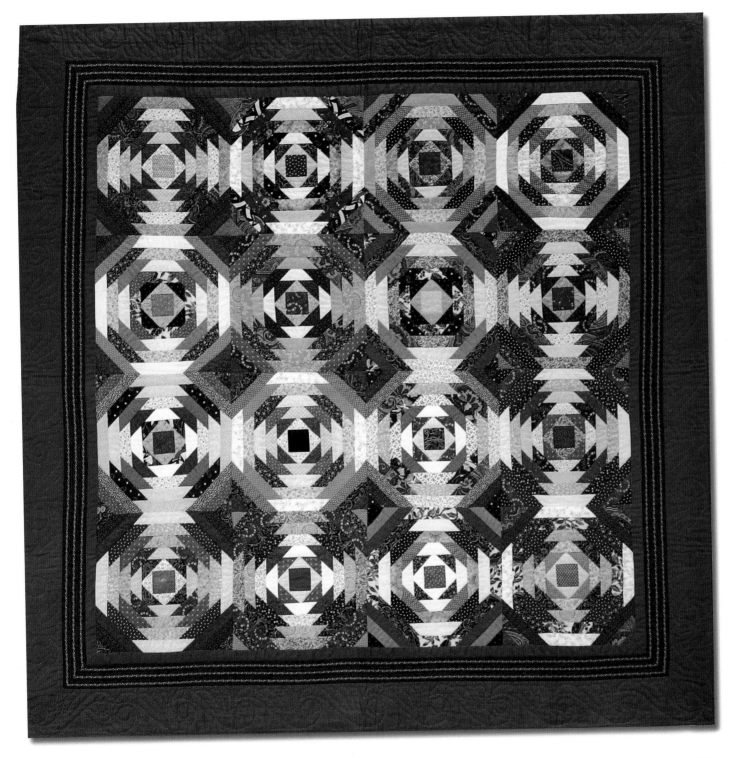

# Shining Star 56" x 56"

## Machine pieced and machine quilted

**W**hat inspired me to make this quilt was an antique quilt with a similar layout. I liked the diagonal flow that was created by the pieced blocks. By the time I made this quilt, I had machine quilted several other quilts and was feeling a little more confident about machine quilting with a contrasting color of thread. When I first started machine quilting I would never have had the guts to do this. I probably would have used a black thread so you could not see my quilting stitches. Don't misunderstand. Black thread would have looked great, but I was ready for some contrast. I love the turquoise thread on the black fabric.

To keep the diagonal flow, I placed a star block in each corner of the border. The three strips line up with the seams on the star block to keep the flow.

# Around the Garden 23" x 58"

*Hand appliquéd, painting on fabric and machine quilted*

I absolutely loved making this quilt. I tried several things I had never attempted before. I saw a method of making insect wings with cake wire and sheer fabric that intrigued me, so I decided to try it and found that it was a lot of fun. I used it on the wings of the bee and the dragonfly. When I was working on the lower block I could not find fabric to get the light and dark blue shading on the flower petals. I wondered if I could paint my own fabric. Sure enough it worked. I was searching through my huge room of fabric (no lie, I have a room) for a pink fabric to use for the Persian Shield leaves. With all the fabric I have I thought surely I would find something that would work, but there was nothing. So again, I decided to paint my own. Now I am finding this painting is too much fun. I do find that I like to paint on the large base fabric in case I mess up I can paint a new leaf or whatever it is that I am painting. I then cut the shape with a seam allowance and appliqué it to the background.

When I reached the border, I liked the idea of repeating the dark fabric but felt it needed just a touch of the light blue sky fabric. Piecing a ¼" strip of the sky blue was just the right amount to pull it all together.

# *NFL Stars* 67" x 67"

## *Machine pieced and machine quilted*

I was asked by a local quilt shop to design a project for a workshop on Super Bowl Sunday. I played around with some pieced block designs and then, finally came to the conclusion that I liked this combination of blocks. I made the decision to use five border strips to pull the darker colors from the center. I often find that I like using two strips of some fabrics on the border as with this project. Using three different widths also helps to add some appeal.

# Black Lone Star 52" x 52"

*Machine pieced and machine quilted*

The idea for this quilt came from the book, "Quilts, Quilts, Quilts." I loved the idea of using star blocks on the border to relate to the larger star in the center. Even though the stars are different styles the theme is carried through to the border using smaller and different types of star blocks. Working with some of the same fabrics from the center star in the border stars helps to create color balance. Personally, I also like that every other block is a solid square and every other block is pieced. Not only do I think it makes a nice layout, but if the size of your pieced blocks is not perfect, you can make adjustments in the solid squares.

# Ponderosa Pine 21" x 27"

*Machine pieced and machine quilted*

This cute little wall quilt was based on a design called "Whispering Pines" by Mumm's The Word pattern company. I loved the use of the strips of fabric around the outer edge. By repeating the colors from the pine trees in the border strips, the project is unified.

# Home is Where the Heart Is 31" x 31"

*Machine pieced, hand appliquéd and machine quilted*

**T**his quilt was just plain fun to make. It is one border after another. It started with the center house being sewn on the machine using paper piecing techniques. The next border was added as a mitered single band, and then I hand appliquéd on the surface. Next, I strip pieced all of the darker fabric to make a frame around the appliqué border. The log cabin block has been and still remains one of my favorite blocks. Before adding the border of log cabin blocks I needed to add a spacer border of a light fabric. Turning the log cabin blocks in different directions created an interesting design on the outer border.

# Snails Trails 84" x 71"

*Machine pieced and machine quilted*

The idea for this quilt came from a commercial pattern designed by Susan Bartlett. Not only did I love the block designs in the center portion of the quilt, but I loved the border idea. What a great concept. Instead of using a single band of fabric around the outside edge, she used scraps of all the darker fabrics. When this quilt was assembled the borders were built right into the rows. Row one was assembled with just border pieces. Row two was a border piece and then, several pieced blocks with another border piece at the other end. So when the rows were assembled, the border was finished. I also think this is a great idea if you don't have enough of one fabric to sew a single band for your border, you could consider piecing a border of scraps.

# Purple Lone Star 38" x 38"

*Machine pieced and hand quilted*

**W**hen I saw this quilt on the cover of Judy Martin's book called "Shining Star Quilts" it was love at first sight. At the time I saw this quilt my local guild, the County Line Quilters, had just selected fabrics for a challenge project. They gave us three fabrics and we were allowed to add three more to make a wall quilt. The problem was I really needed seven fabrics. My first impression was to dye the light print to a shade of purple. But what you need to know is that I did not know anything about fabric dying. But I thought, how hard could that be? Well, all day long I experimented with different dyes on scraps of the light print fabric. When my husband, Joe, got home from work he said "What did you do today?" A normal question as he has always shown an interest in

my work. But I had nothing to show. I was bummed. I had spent the entire day trying to dye a color that I never got. Joe said, "The back of that dark purple print you are using is the exact color you are trying to dye." Here I had wasted the entire day, and the color I needed was simply the back of a fabric I already had. Now, I try to remember to ask Joe before he leaves for work if he has any brilliant ideas! He often does.

One of the things I loved about this border is that it was pieced into the design. Rather than adding two strips of fabric as bands to create another border, the strips were built into the triangles. Brilliant idea.

# Joe's Quilt 45" x 45"

*Machine pieced and hand quilted with lots of love*

One day my husband commented that I had not made him a quilt. Even though I had made many quilts for our beds and walls, Joe felt he needed one to hang on his office wall. When I started looking for ideas, I saw this design in Quiltmaker magazine. I liked the way the triangles from the lattice strips were added to the borders to complete the design. The way the pattern was designed the triangles were pieced into a strip of fabric and then, an outer border strip was added. If I had this border to do over I would have cut one strip and appliquéd the border triangles. Next time I will know better. But think how unbalanced the border would be if those triangles were not added.

As I was selecting the fabrics for this quilt, a customer of mine came into the shop. She asked what I was doing, and I told her I was making a quilt for Joe. She said, "I want to purchase a yard and a quarter of that paisley print." I asked her what she planned on doing with it. She told me that she was going to make a tie for Joe. Suzy made the tie for Joe which he wears to the office where his quilt hangs on the wall. Now that is pretty coordinated.

# Mariner's Star 88"x 88"

*Hand and machine pieced (mostly hand), hand appliquéd and hand quilted*

The idea for this quilt started with a pattern by Mary Kay Ryan. When I saw the pattern I fell in love with it. I particularly liked how border print fabrics were used in the design. I got to work fussy cutting each piece of fabric so the border print fabric would come together to create interesting designs. As you view the quilt, the on-point center portion was where the pattern ended. When I reached the edge of the pattern I had this feeling that it was not finished. But I was unsure how to proceed. I pinned the center portion onto a wooden slat on the ceiling molding in my sewing room and started on another project. I hated not finishing. I am a finisher. I start one project and finish it before starting on the next. I do not feel that other people need to work the way I do. But as I was growing up my mother always made us finish everything so I feel guilty if I don't finish. (Blame it on your mother!) A few days after pinning the design on the boards, I walked into the room and one of the push pins had fallen out and the design was hanging on point. I loved it. I got out my table paper and started designing corner units. After the corners were sewn and I was ready to design a border, it just seemed like the border design should have elements that were on-point to complement the center.

I was very honored when this quilt won a special award for Pennsylvania artists and hung in my Senator's office in Washington D.C. for one year. The Senator's wife told me that since quilts give a soothing feeling and often create a calming effect, they hung it in the debate room.

# Flowers and Friends I 88" x 88"

*Hand appliquéd and hand quilted*

Even though I don't enjoy gardening, I do enjoy seeing beautiful flower gardens. I decided to create my garden from fabric, and it blossomed into a garden of delight. The first block I designed for this project was what I refer to as "Heard it Through the Grapevine". (Block in the top, right corner.) I began offering it as a one day workshop to teach the appliqué techniques that work well for me. It became my most requested class. I knew then that I had to design more blocks for a larger garden. I photographed flowers and studied flower books for ideas. For contrast with the smooth lines of the appliqué I added the rigid lines of the star. As I was sewing the center I kept thinking that I wanted a dark blue border. But if I appliquéd with the same fabrics I used in the center and put them on a dark background I would lose the contrast. I had to come up with a light area on which to appliqué. Thinking about the points of the star and the simplicity of the half square triangle I drafted this border. By turning the half square triangles I could create this zig-zag design. The light area was the perfect place to repeat the appliqué shapes used in the center blocks. You will also notice the spacer border between the main part of the quilt and the zig-zag design. In the "Determining the Size of the Units/Blocks" section of this book, I explained how the spacer strip may be needed to get a half square triangle shape that was easy to cut. That was the case with this border.

# Caribbean Floral Fantasy 98" x 98"'

*Hand appliquéd, machine pieced and hand quilted*

**Y**et another trip to the Caribbean inspired this quilt. The warm breezes through the palms, the lush colors of the flora and the hues of the sea all enriched the making of this quilt. I was in the mood for purple and, of course, what I consider to be the worlds' best neutral, green. My original plan was to appliqué the center medallion and then, I had no idea what I was going to do next. After the center appliqué area was complete I turned it on point and thought "OK, I like that". Then I had to design corners. I got out my table paper and cut triangles the size I would need. I drew lots of designs before I realized most of what I was drawing was going to be far too busy. I needed to simplify. I love making log cabin blocks. Using these blocks I could create a nice line in the design of the blocks to play off of the on-point center. When it came to the borders, I knew miniature log cabin blocks were going to be part of the design. With the right placement I could open up a light area to appliqué the flowers. Think of how different this border would look if I allowed a seam to stop me. The flowers would have ended at the edge of the log cabin blocks. By modifying the flower from the center and taking it across the seams on the border, a wonderful balance was created.

# Feathered Star 24"x 24"

*Machine pieced by Janet Shultzabarger, hand appliquéd and hand quilted by author*

**T**his little wall quilt was a sample block from a larger quilt that Janet and I designed for our guild's raffle project. We decided to make a smaller version of the larger quilt. The intention was that the person who sold the most raffle tickets would win this little quilt. Guess what? I sold the most raffle tickets and ended up with the wall quilt. I love the combination of the feathered star with the appliqué border. By pulling all the colors from the center onto the border the project is cohesive. This wonderful little wall quilt hangs in my office, and I enjoy looking at it every single day.

# Another Day in Paradise 80" x 80"

*Hand appliquéd and hand quilted*

**V**isits to Mexico make me long for the warm sunshine during the gray days of winter. Using soothing tropical colors and a bold design allowed me to escape Pennsylvania's cold winter days. Although I may not be in the sun, I am allowed to bask in my warm thoughts. This was my second medallion style quilt. I was searching for a way to achieve balance in the design by using the two main colors in the border. The whole time I was sewing on this quilt I was at a loss for a good name for this project. During the hand quilting I heard a song by the Eagles called "Another Day in Paradise". The Eagles are my all-time favorite band, and the title of their song seemed a perfect fit because this quilt will always remind me of trips to Mexico and the warm sunshine.

# Earthly Delights 81" x 81"

*Hand appliqués and hand quilted*

Inspired by a 19th century design by Friedrick Fischback, this quilt's earth tones have the feeling of early autumn when nights are cool, flowers are still blooming and leaves are beginning to fall. I remember picking these fabrics as though it was yesterday. I had completed the appliqué in the center and was deciding which fabric I wanted for what I refer to as the overlay fabric. It would become a major part of the project. I had it narrowed down to two choices, one being a brown fabric, the other a pink fabric. I asked several friends which one they liked better. A quote I heard goes like this, "Why do we ask for advice when we already know the answer?" All along I knew I would use the brown, but sometimes I need to hear reinforcement. Think how different this would have looked if the pink fabric had been used instead of the brown. In order to unify the project I used scallops on the border. It helped to pull the curves from the center to the outside. Repeating the colors and shapes (modified in size) from the center, I achieved the balance I desired. I feel good whenever I look at this quilt. It soothes my soul.

# Bright Hopes 88" x 88"

*Hand appliquéd and machine quilted*

The inspiration for this quilt came from a Damask white-on-white table cloth design. Memories of when I started to design this quilt are not good ones. I was just in the beginning stages of drawing when terrorists ravaged our country on 9/11. I cried a lot, and the designing took much longer than normal as I grieved for the families of the victims. I did not have a color theme in mind but as the design was growing I kept thinking there had to be brighter days ahead. I knew then this quilt had to be on a black background with the brightest colors I could find. Many elements from the center were redesigned to fit into the border plan. As with the design of this quilt, our country unified and grew stronger.

# Midnight Floral Fantasy 98"x98"

*Hand and machine appliquéd and machine quilted*

For several years I designed the raffle quilt for my guild, the Letort Quilters. Our guild does a large quilt project with the proceeds going to local charities. A friend of mine, Janet Shultzabarger, who owns the local quilt shop, Calico Corners, and I designed the quilt together. Our guild has always preferred to have some piecing and some appliqué on the raffle quilt. Placing the pineapple log cabin blocks in the corners created a nice movement to the quilt. The borders repeat many of the elements used in the center medallion. On the original quilt approximately 30 guild members helped to make the project. I liked the results so much that I had to make one for myself.

# Memories of the Holidays 88" x 88"

*Hand appliquéd, hand embroidered and machine quilted*

The idea of making a Christmas medallion quilt had been stewing in my brain for many years. Before I started designing, I wrote about fifteen different words of items that reminded me of the holidays. I knew this would give me inspiration while I was drawing. When I finally got out the paper and started to draw, everything just fell into place. When I started to sew the hand embroidery for the pine needles I remembered a student of mine telling me how nice it looked to combine two strands of embroidery floss in two different shades of one color to create more interest. She was so right. The pine needles came to life with a combination of four shades of green. After I had the first border completed I placed it along the edge of the quilt. Immediately I knew it needed more red. I placed some small scraps of red circles on the surface and came to the conclusion each border needed another fifty circles. I often tell people I like including circles in my quilts, but I must admit that I was a little tired of making all those little circles by the time I had finished these borders. Adding a red flange along each border also helped to balance the amount of red needed on the borders.

# Sunny Side Up 47"x 102"

*Hand appliquéd, hand beaded and machine quilted*

This quilt was inspired by Indian fiber art. Since many of the Indian arts incorporate beading I wanted to include beading in my work as well. This quilt is my attempt to merge the Eastern influence with a splash of bright colors. I have been fascinated with beads for many years and often purchased beads at trade shows knowing that some day I would use lots of them in a quilt. I accomplished my mission on this quilt. When I made the decision to incorporate beading in this project I had the help of two friends. One was Mary Stori who has written several books on beading and another was the owner of a beading shop, Amy Cline. Both Mary and Amy were a huge help to me during the many, many hours that I spent hand beading. I was thrilled with the result. The border consists of three bands of fabric with a flange on each side and, of course, many of appliqué shapes modified from the center of the quilt.

# Buckley Album Quilt 74" x 74"

*Hand appliquéd, ink drawings by Joe Buckley, and hand quilted*

The inspiration for this quilt began when I saw Elly Sienkiewicz's book, "Baltimore Beauties and Beyond." I made several blocks from the book and then designed a few of my own. When I was researching Baltimore Album quilts, I found that the original makers liked to incorporate things from their lives into their blocks. I liked the idea and wanted to have pictures drawn on my blocks but was afraid to draw them myself with a permanent marker. My husband, Joe, said he would do it for me. After the appliqué was completed Joe did the ink drawing on each block. Each block has a drawing of something that was important in our lives, like our first meeting at Lock Haven State College, our birthdates, our anniversary, etc. One of my favorite stories to tell about this quilt is when it was hanging in a quilt show. Two ladies were walking by the quilt and one lady said to her friend, "Look at the drawings on those blocks." The other person stated with a great deal of authority, "That is just preprinted fabric." She was not whispering, and I could not help but overhear her comment. I thought about walking away, but I just had to say something. I said, "Excuse me, but I could not help but overhear your comments. This is my quilt, and my husband did all of those drawings. He would be honored that you thought his work was that good." Neither lady knew what to say but the first lady had a smile on her face to indicate to her friend, so I guess you don't know every thing! I still smile when I think of it.

When I reached the borders I knew I wanted to do something personal. Outside our kitchen window stood this beautiful Bing cherry tree. I cut my table paper to the needed size and drew a branch with leaves and cherries. My original plan was to use the cherry border on all sides but after I finished the second border and put it on the side of the quilt I did not like it. It took me a long time to figure out what I did not like about it, but finally I figured out the reason. Cherry branches grow horizontally and not vertically. When the branches were placed vertically on the quilt it did not feel nor look right. I then decided to make grape borders for the two sides as grapes vines would grow vertically. I loved making the two different borders yet creating a fabulous balance to the entire project. After the borders were attached and the miters were sewn I decided to appliqué a few additional leaves so they crossed over in the lattice and one grape leaf over each mitered seam.

# Red Dragon 42"x 60"

*Hand appliquéd and machine quilted*

This was the first quilt that I ventured to design on my own. Prior to this, most of my quilts were made from commercial patterns or traditional quilt designs.

One year for Christmas a friend mailed a card with a black and white sketch of a dragon on the front. She had been traveling with a choral group through China and mailed the dragon card instead of a traditional Christmas card. I liked the dragon design and held onto the card for years. I had no idea why I was holding on to it until one day I pulled the card out from the back of a drawer. I started thinking about how I could take the dragon design and turn it into a quilt. I began to draw but was unsure of how to get the shading I wanted on the dragon. I was lucky enough to know the local high school art teacher, Denny Zeigler. I called Denny and asked if he could give me some advice. It took him all of five minutes to show me what was needed. I was so impressed. After I had the dragon appliquéd I started playing on paper with border ideas. I thought of the arches when you walk into Chinatown. They are a shiny gold and have very ornate designs. I did not think I had the ability to sew anything quite so intricate so I opted to do a modified version.

When I got to the top border of the quilt I had to do a little research. I went to the library at Dickinson College. I found two books with Chinese characters. When I went to check the books out from the library the librarian asked what I was doing with those books. I thought it a rather odd question. After all, I was at the library and I was checking out some books. But I told her that I was doing some research for a quilt project. I then asked her why she wanted to know what I was doing with the books, and she said "No one has checked out those books for 12 years". So, she had a good reason to ask the question. The librarian then introduced me to an exchange student from China to confirm that I had found the correct character for dragon. I used lamé in a reverse appliqué technique for the Chinese characters and the area on the side borders.

# Wagner's Bridge 62" x 76"

*Hand appliquéd, machine embroidered and machine quilted*

This quilt has such fond memories for me. One year on my birthday my husband asked what I wanted to do. I said that I loved the covered bridges he had taken me to on previous occasions, but that I had never photographed them. And what I really wanted to do was to take a drive back over Sherman's Creek and photograph the bridges. The center portion of this quilt comes from two of those photographs. I took several photographs that day and really liked two different pictures. I knew I had to choose one. I decided on Wagner's Bridge but used flowers from the front of one of the other pictures. As I was appliquéing the center, I kept seeing a stone wall in my mind. I wondered if I could make the quilt appear as though the viewer was looking through a stone window. This border was one of the easiest borders I have ever appliquéd. I cut a wide strip of beige fabric, later known as the mortar fabric and appliquéd large rock shapes on the surface. Do you know how freeing it is to make rocks? There is no wrong size or method for making a rock. You can always say you wanted that sharp point on an otherwise smooth rock. Who would know the difference? Having a blank stone wall seemed rather boring so I drew a grape vine with some grape clusters and began to sew. The end result is one my favorite quilts. I am really glad my husband took me to see all of those covered bridges over the years because it led to this picturesque quilt.

# Biography

Karen began quilting in 1982 through an adult education program. She started by making a king sized bed quilt and was immediately addicted to quilting. She made many projects for friends and family and has worked with her local quilt guild, the LeTort Quilters, since they first organized in 1984. In April of 1986 Karen received her first quilting award. J.C. Penney organized a quilt block contest and Karen won first place at the local level, then the regional level, and onto the national level. The block was joined into a quilt along with 15 other blocks and exhibited at the Great American Quilt Show in New York City. In the fall of 1986 Karen's husband, Joe, was offered a job in the Philadelphia area. To entice Karen to move Joe said, "Why don't you open your own quilt shop?" On November 29, 1986 Karen opened The Country Quilt Shop. The shop was a huge success. Karen began developing her own classes. She entered her first major quilt competition in the spring of 1991. The "Dragon" quilt received a first place in one show and a second place in another show. It was truly the start of Karen designing her own quilts and entering many more shows. Since that first quilt competition Karen's quilts have won many local and national awards including seven Best of Show awards. In the spring of 1992 her first book "From Basics To Binding: A Complete Guide To Making Quilts" was published. She has since published three other books, "Above & Beyond Basics", "Love to Quilt...Bears, Bears, Bears" and "Applique Basics: Flower Wreaths". In May of 1992 Karen had her first cover quilt and since that time has had twelve more quilts appear on the cover of major quilting magazines. Karen is very passionate about what she does. She loves designing her quilts and sharing her tips and tricks with all her students.

If you would like more information about Karen, her classes and her quilts visit her web site at **www.karenkaybuckley.com**.

Boy do I love my work,
and it certainly has brought me an
abundance of success.  Not just in the awards I have won
and the positive comments from those who have
viewed my art, but mostly in the friends I have
made. My life has been greatly
enriched by all of them.